The INSIDER'S GUIDE to
Working with Universities

The

Practical Insights for Board Members, Businesspeople, Entrepreneurs, Philanthropists, Alumni, Parents, and Administrators

Insider's Guide to Working with Universities

JAMES W. DEAN JR. & DEBORAH Y. CLARKE

THE UNIVERSITY OF NORTH CAROLINA PRESS

Chapel Hill

This book was published with the assistance of the Luther H. Hodges Sr. and Luther H. Hodges Jr. Fund of the University of North Carolina Press.

Set in Utopia and TheSans by Tseng Information Systems, Inc.
Manufactured in the United States of America

The University of North Carolina Press has been a member
of the Green Press Initiative since 2003.

Jacket photograph of lecture room © iStockphoto.com/Pixelci.

Library of Congress Cataloging-in-Publication Data
Names: Dean, James W., Jr., 1956– author. | Clarke, Deborah Y., 1971– author.
Title: The insider's guide to working with universities : practical insights for board members, businesspeople, entrepreneurs, philanthropists, alumni, parents, and administrators / James W. Dean Jr. and Deborah Y. Clarke.
Description: Chapel Hill : The University of North Carolina Press, [2019] | Includes bibliographical references and index.
Identifiers: LCCN 2019011633 | ISBN 9781469653419 (cloth : alk. paper) | ISBN 9781469653426 (ebook)
Subjects: LCSH: College trustees—United States. | Universities and colleges—United States—Administration. | Universities and colleges—United States—Business management.
Classification: LCC LB2342.5 .D43 2019 | DDC 378.1/011—dc23
LC record available at https://lccn.loc.gov/2019011633

To
Jan, Noelle, and Bridget
and
Walt, Emma Kate, and Redding

Contents

Figures, Tables, and Graph

The INSIDER'S GUIDE to Working with Universities

Introduction

"*I know so much that I don't know where to begin.*"

I.1. *Source*: James Stevenson/The New Yorker Collection/The Cartoon Bank.

We wrote *The Insider's Guide to Working with Universities* to help businesspeople, particularly board members and new academic leaders, who work with colleges and universities. This book will give them a clearer and more comprehensive understanding of how higher education works, and it will help them perform better in their university-related roles. American colleges and universities enroll more than 20 million students,[1] and more than a third of U.S. adults have earned at least a bachelor's degree.[2] Higher education is tied inextricably to this country's history, public discourse, scientific discovery and innovation, dissemination of knowledge, and, perhaps most notably, our well-being and prosperity.[3] The affection of alumni for their alma maters is unique to American colleges and universities. Visitors to the United States often are amazed at the common practice of proudly displaying the name of one's college on sweatshirts and bumper stickers. For many reasons, the academic sector[4] is fundamental to the U.S. economy and culture; it is difficult to imagine our country without it.

But higher education also faces a wide array of issues and problems. Many institutions have trouble matching revenues and expenses. Some struggle to convince the public of their value and relevance. Others seem to take too long to make important decisions and thus miss fleeting opportunities. Many have ample faculty available to teach courses of limited interest to students but few instructors to teach courses in great demand. A number of colleges and universities deliberate over how and even whether to implement new technologies. All of these problems are similar to many of the problems that businesses face. It seems logical that colleges and universities could benefit greatly from people who bring business experience and insight to their campuses.

To illustrate the struggles that colleges and universities face, consider a recent article in the *Chronicle of Higher Education*, which describes a set of problems facing the University of Maine.[5] The dwindling number of high school graduates in the state makes it hard to enroll enough students and to support the full range of educational offerings the university has historically provided. There is redundancy among the offerings of the different institutions in the Maine university system, which is difficult to rationalize for both bureaucratic and political reasons. This situation is similar in many ways to challenges faced by businesses in declining markets and again would seem ripe for leveraging the experience of businesspeople.

Beyond the specific issues faced by colleges and universities, institutions of higher learning increasingly are expected to help address serious and complex matters in their states or regions, or even national and international problems such as poverty, hunger, climate change, and infectious diseases.[6] The academy is seen as possessing the expertise and scope to solve such problems. But implementing and scaling effective solutions to these (and even much simpler) issues requires operational and managerial expertise more often found in businesses.

Many college graduates go to work for business organizations. Business majors have been popular for some time,[7] and students who study arts and sciences often gravitate toward businesses for their first jobs and beyond. The counsel of businesspeople once again seems well worth considering on the question of how best to prepare college graduates to be successful for their future roles.

And in fact, many businesspeople step forward to support academic institutions as they address these issues and problems. Their support takes various forms, but they can most often be found serving on the governing boards of academic institutions. As we prepared to write this book, we talked to a number of businesspeople. Here are some of their stories:

1. A new board member at a private university in the Northeast, of which she is an alumna, was at a presentation of the university's plans for a capital campaign. She had little experience in fund-raising but has had a successful international career in operations with a Fortune 500 corporation. She was concerned that the rate at which the university was progressing would not allow it to achieve its goals and asked the presenters about the run rate of meetings and proposals. She said they looked at her "like she had six heads." As this was one of her first board meetings, she was quite shaken up by the others' reaction and questioned her ability to add value to the board when the administrators didn't even understand her questions.

2. An alumnus of a public university in the South, graduating with an engineering degree several decades ago, has had a very successful career in private equity and was asked to join the board of the engineering school at his alma mater. He had high hopes for his ability to help his school, and presumably the school had high hopes for his financial support. He was particularly excited when the school announced it was moving aggressively into distance education. After two years, however, he was disappointed that the school had not accomplished much in this area. He stepped down from the board and reduced his contacts with his alma mater.

3. At a public university in the Midwest, the board became concerned about the level of risk—financial, strategic, and operational—to which the university was exposed. Board members initiated a project to better understand and holistically manage the risks found across the university. A board member

with considerable relevant business experience was named project manager. Senior academic leaders (deans, vice presidents) were directed to participate in the project and were organized into working groups to address specific types of risk. While it was difficult to get these busy individuals in the same room to meet, each group eventually produced its report. The second stage of the project was to pull together these reports into an overall report for the university. After a long process of revision, the report was finished, printed, and presented at a board meeting, and the participants were thanked. But the board member who led the effort described the process as "messy and inefficient" and was surprised that university leaders were initially either reluctant or unable to spend time on the project. He said, "As a businessperson, you're used to having people who handle operational level things, but this was not the case here." More troubling is, despite the fact that the report took more than a year to produce and its cost ran well into the hundreds of thousands of dollars, it had no discernible impact on the university.

We have worked throughout our careers with groups charged with overseeing universities, including boards of governors, trustees, and visitors. Like the people in these stories, most of the members of these groups are businesspeople. Here are some of the questions they have asked us:

- Why do decisions in universities take so long?
- What is tenure? Are all faculty tenured? How do you get tenure?
- When faculty members act out, why don't you simply fire them?
- Are research grants like earmarks, so you don't have to compete for them?
- Why isn't growth a priority for universities, as it is for businesses?

These stories and questions tell us that many members of university boards have had limited prior exposure to higher education, and thus they lack deep understanding of the institutions they are responsible for overseeing.[8] Boards make important decisions about strategic priorities, senior-level hiring, and budgets. They link the university to the broader community, citizens, and alumni. Their understanding of how universities work is critical to the success of the colleges and universities that they serve. The stakes are high:

- miscommunication and confusion on the part of board members and administrators
- each group erroneously concluding that the other is incompetent
- alumni leaving their boards and distancing themselves from their alma maters
- missed opportunities to leverage board members' knowledge and experience
- uninformed decisions due to a misunderstanding of how colleges and universities work
- significant time and money wasted on ill-conceived projects
- a damaged reputation resulting from frustrations expressed outside the institution

Based on these significant stakes, we decided to write a book that explains to these important individuals how colleges and universities work so they can make these institutions better. Our primary audience is people who serve on boards, which may be at the institutional level (for example, boards of trustees or foundation boards), at a professional school (for example, law, medicine, or journalism), or at a center or institute (such as a center for ethics or the environment). Frequently, board members are alumni of the institutions they serve, and they are not paid for their often-considerable efforts. They typically are highly motivated to serve because they care deeply about the college they once attended.

We also intend for this book to help businesspeople who take on senior positions *inside* universities, perhaps as a dean or even as president. People who accept these roles have to learn a great deal very quickly. Many institutions have hired businesspeople in senior roles over the past few years, including presidents at the University of Oklahoma,[9] the University of Iowa, Mt. St. Mary's College, Vanderbilt University, and the University of Montana.[10] In fact, a recent study finds that about 40 percent of college presidents have never held a tenured or tenure-track faculty position.[11] I (JD) have hired several deans with nonacademic backgrounds, all of whom have remarked on the significant challenge of understanding how things work in higher education.

In *Governance Reconsidered*, former university president Susan Resneck Pierce recounts numerous stories of nontraditional college presidents (with business backgrounds) whose lack of knowledge of academics made their transition and time as president much more difficult, and in some cases led to their dismissal. Some ignored the faculty; others did not expect their decisions to be questioned; still others made big decisions with no awareness of the need for shared governance (see chapter 6). A former oil industry CEO, hired to become the first new president at the University of Oklahoma in more than two decades, laid off six senior administrators on his first day on the job. "Although some expected the new president to sweep in and clean house, [James L.] Gallogly's background as a business leader and the suddenness of his broad staffing moves mean Oklahoma is now a prime example of issues arising when a university hires a president from a nontraditional background who goes on to execute the leadership transition in a way perceived as unusual," reported *Inside Higher Ed*.[12] Time will tell whether these swift organizational changes, made without consultation with the university's board or the faculty senate, will negatively impact President Gallogly's performance. Regardless, as Pierce asserts, a clearer and more grounded understanding of academic organizations and practices leads to greater success for university leaders.[13]

A third audience for this book is potential college and university donors, for whom a better understanding of academic institutions could help to shape their philanthropy. Much of the knowledge that potential donors have, such as the priorities of the dean or president, comes from information shared by university development officers. But it is difficult for prospective donors to appreciate how (or even whether) their gifts will actually drive institutional priorities without understanding their organizational context. Fund-raisers who come from outside higher education may also benefit from deeper knowledge of how these institutions operate.

A fourth group is businesspeople nearing retirement who dream of college teaching. Many businesspeople would love to share with young people what they have learned in their careers, and some have made a substantial impact. We have encountered such individuals in business schools, as well as in economics, chemistry, and public health. But many become disenchanted with their new institutions, partially due to an incomplete understanding of just what they have gotten themselves into.

A fifth audience is lawmakers and legislators, especially at the state level, who are responsible for public funding of higher education. Financial support for public colleges and universities varies across states, but this support is absolutely critical to these institutions.[14] Higher education is the third-largest category in state general fund budgets[15] (the portion financed primarily by taxes), after K–12 education and Medicaid. Still, state funding for public higher education has dropped precipitously over the past decade. According to a report by the American Academy of Arts and Sciences, "Measured in inflation-adjusted dollars per full-time equivalent (FTE) student, states have been cutting support for well over a decade, and spending cuts accelerated in response to the Great Recession. Between 2008 and 2013, states cut appropriation support per FTE student in the median public research university by more than 26 percent (overall, support per FTE student at the median public institution was cut by more than 20 percent)."[16]

Our final audience is those in the industries, including consulting firms and online education partners, whose customers are colleges and universities. Many of these enterprises were started by former insiders who do understand universities, but any academic leader can recall excruciating sales presentations completely lacking in an understanding of academic culture. We once suffered through a presentation by a sales representative who didn't appreciate the give-and-take nature of academic discussions (or, for that matter, of effective sales presentations in any setting). He was still engaged in his monologue, aided by dozens of PowerPoint slides, at minute fifty-six of a sixty-minute meeting. No sale.

This is not meant to be a criticism of businesspeople's knowledge or willingness to learn. "It cannot be taken for granted that trustees will assume their offices with a robust understanding of and appreciation for the core mission of a university," writes Keith Whittington for the *Chronicle of Higher Education.* "They rarely have the scholarly training or experience of a faculty member, and their professional experience often derives from institutions and environments that have little in common with the world of academe."[17] To the contrary, we wrote this book because businesspeople add tremendous value to the academic enterprise, particularly because of the diverse experiences and perspectives that they bring.

But it is difficult to understand the practices of institutions that one did not grow up in, and often people judge new and unfamiliar organizations by the standards that they already know.[18] People from entrepreneurial environments often find corporate life incredibly constricting ("You have rules for everything"), while those comfortable in established firms find the start-up life to be painfully chaotic ("Is anyone in charge of anything?"). Similar challenges can be found in transitions between American and European organizations ("Do I really have to shake everyone's hand, every day?") and between more and less regulated industries.

The differences between academic and business organizations are at least as significant as these. We suggest that businesspeople think of academic organizations as if they were in a different industry in a different country. Yet businesspeople often take important university roles with relatively little experience and knowledge of how these organizations work. This point also applies to nontraditional academic leaders, as well as to donors, teachers, and vendors. It is curious that organizations dedicated to education often fail to educate the very people most interested in helping them.

This is not a new phenomenon, as Samuel Cohen explains: more than 100 years ago, notable economist and sociologist Thorstein Veblen (who wrote about America's "leisure class" and coined the term "conspicuous consumption") penned a book critical of universities run by businesspeople. His original attempt to publish the book was quashed by the businesspeople running his university, the University of Missouri at Columbia. Even Veblen "was of course not so naïve as to think that large operations that involve lots of money don't need people with appropriate expertise." But he objected to the limited appreciation of businesspeople for "esoteric knowledge," a complaint that would likely find many supporters among today's academics.[19]

Similarly, Francis Wayland, who in 1955 was president of Brown University, asked, "How can colleges prosper, directed by men, very good men to be sure, but who know about every other thing except about education?"[20] While today there certainly are more women, not just men, serving on university boards, unfortunately not much else has changed.

Most people who don't work inside universities see them through a few limited prisms. For example, their undergraduate classroom experience gives them some (perhaps dated) idea of one important element of universities.[21] Many have a romanticized notion based on their own experiences, perhaps accompanied by an understanding of the faculty that is to some degree a caricature.[22] A savvy former board member told us that "your personal experience is going to get in the way if you're not careful. The university is much more than your undergraduate experience, and even that may have changed."[23] (See chapter 3.) This theme of recalling vivid memories of one's own college days was raised by another experienced board member, who said that it may lead people to have an excessive focus on undergraduate education and to neglect to ask difficult questions, especially regarding the research enterprise.[24]

Many people are fans of college athletics, which sensitizes them to the galvanizing effect of school spirit, the stakes of student-athlete recruiting, and the complexity of athletic and academic eligibility. Also, most businesspeople have some awareness of the research conducted in universities: that some of it takes place in laboratories, that some of it sounds interesting and some of it useless, and that it occasionally results in accolades and awards such as the Nobel Prize. Finally, most businesspeople have had experience hiring new college graduates, so they have a rough sense of what these individuals know and don't know. Yet all of these experiences taken together, while generally helpful, leave a great deal for businesspeople to learn about colleges and universities. Due to the lack of understanding of academic institutions, businesspeople are tempted to see them simply as badly run businesses, with costs that are too high, decisions that take too long, and no clear sense of their objectives. While there is some truth to each of these observations, a more complete grasp of the nature of colleges and universities should help businesspeople to fulfill their responsibilities more effectively.

We will attempt to convey in the following chapters that, rather than being poor imitations of for-profit businesses, colleges and universities are fundamentally different types of organizations.[25] As Jim Collins of *Good to Great* fame put it, "We must reject the idea—well-intentioned, but dead wrong—that the primary path to greatness in the social sectors [including universities] is to become 'more like a business.'"[26]

Academic institutions have very different missions, values, and goals. This does *not* mean that business principles and tools have no place in universities; colleges and universities have in fact used such business tools extensively and effectively. It does mean, however, that approaching academic leadership with a purely business mindset—without understanding the differences between sectors—is likely to be unsuccessful, even with the best of intentions.

With all of this in mind, we have a few requests for you, our readers, as you make your way through the rest of the book:

1. Remember that colleges and universities can be better, and you can help make them better.
2. Please suspend disbelief and skepticism as you read. Not everything that drives you crazy about universities *should* drive you crazy. There are good reasons for some practices that initially seem strange.
3. You know how to learn quickly about new companies and industries. Put these skills to work in reading this book and in your interactions with your college or university.[27]
4. Universities, even American universities, have been around for centuries. While the mindset that this longevity creates can be a source of frustration for fast-moving business executives (and in some cases it should), consider that sustained success counts for something.
5. Keep in mind that, for all its problems and faults, the American system of higher education is the most successful in the world. For example, 58 percent of students who leave their home country to study abroad come to the United States.[28] This collective market share would be envied by most American industries. You can use this book to explore why this approach has been successful, as well as what its limits are.

None of this means that colleges and universities cannot be improved; they can and, in fact, they must. Academic institutions face a wide range of vexing problems. Board members and other college and university leaders from business absolutely need to help us solve them. We hope that this book will help them collaborate with academic institutions more effectively and with less wasted effort.

We have organized the subsequent chapters to build knowledge and understanding of how American colleges and universities work and how this information relates directly to the impact that businesspeople can make. The topics in this book are connected to one another in complex ways. For example, university goals and budget systems are related to organizational structure and faculty research. While we have laid the book out in the most logical way we could think of, we have also included many cross-chapter references to point out these connections.

In chapter 1, we discuss the most important similarities and differences between businesses and academic organizations. In chapter 2, we explore the differences *among* various academic institutions, including private versus public, and the different market segments that institutions target. Chapter 3 goes inside academic institutions and describes the schools, centers, degree programs, and administrative units that make them up, as well as the ways in which college teaching has been recently recreated. In chapter 4, we describe the many ways in which higher education institutions are influenced from the outside, including by federal and state governments, court decisions, and accreditors. Chapter 5 focuses on the faculty, including how they earned their doctor of philosophy (PhD) degrees, and the differences between tenure-track and non-tenure-track professors. In chapter 6, we explore the organizational structure of universities, including the professional affiliations of leaders at different levels and how they exert influence, and we provide an overview of faculty governance. Chapter 7 explains the nature of university research in various fields, how it is funded, and the management and monetization of intellectual property. Chapter 8 deals with the finances of colleges and universities, including sources and uses of funding. Finally, we draw on all of this information in chapter 9 to make recommendations for how to more effectively help academic institutions through board service or other leadership roles.

How Are Businesses and Universities Different? How Are They Similar?

I have no illusion that universities somehow evade the logic of the marketplace. But no other institution is designed so intentionally to provide structures in which free intellectual inquiry can take place. —Lisi Schoenbach

As businesspeople begin their work with academic organizations, the wisest among them proceed with caution to understand the lay of the land. As they gradually become familiar with universities through their roles as trustees or leaders, they come to understand certain key similarities and differences between business and academe. This chapter addresses these similarities and differences. Of course, there are many differences among businesses as well as among colleges and universities, so we will focus on the most widely shared characteristics of each.

How Are Businesses and Universities Different?

GOALS

Businesses have many goals, but the most fundamental is profit. Other goals such as market share, operating efficiency, and talent retention are all in service of long-term profitability. Profit is what allows a business to survive, to invest in growth, and to provide its owners— whether private or public—with a return on their investment. The profit goal is so fundamental to business that its pursuit is used to differentiate between those organizations considered businesses and those that are not—that is, nonprofits.

There is no goal in academic organizations equivalent to profit.[1] This is one of the most profound differences between the two types of organizations and, as we will see, the root of many other differences. Colleges and universities are driven by their missions, which are focused on some combination of teaching, research, and public service. An institution's pursuit of its mission—such as creating new knowledge, educating future leaders, finding cures, disseminating research for the public good, achieving new insight into social change, contributing to economic impact, and so on—characterizes an important driver of higher education.

Despite this focus on mission, no single objective is shared by everyone in the academic institution.[2] Each constituency within the academy has a nuanced idea about the relative importance of teaching, research, and service, as well as how each should be measured. In making plans or decisions, "What are we trying to accomplish?" is as important a question as "Will this help us get there?" It is impossible to overstate this fundamental point in understanding the differences between businesses and academic organizations and how little it is understood or appreciated outside the academic sector. Another way of making this point is that academic missions work well at the level of philosophy but are much less effective than profit as a guide to decision-making. This is despite the real, tangible commitment to missions that is easily perceived on college campuses.

The closest that colleges come to a bottom line is the pursuit of something that could be called prestige, reputation, or quality.[3] While quality refers to the actual excellence of one element of the mission (for example, undergraduate education), prestige and reputation are indirect results of quality. The better an academic organization executes any of its core functions, the better its reputation will likely be, all things being equal. But of course, all things are never equal; reputation can, for example, be influenced by strategic communications, in which universities are increasingly investing. And, just as in business, reputations are nearly always lagging indicators of quality. An institution on the way up is probably better than its reputation, while one on the way down is probably worse.

Despite these nuances, reputation and prestige are so important because they strengthen the very things that create quality, particularly students, faculty, and donor support. In this way universities are like their athletic teams—the best are able to recruit the best coaches and athletes and to sustain their dominance—and are the opposite of professional sports, where the worst teams get the best draft picks. In academics, the rich get richer, both literally and figuratively.[4]

Further emphasizing this difference in goals between businesses

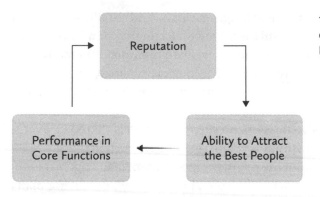

1.1. Reputation as the cause and outcome of high performance.

and academic organizations is the measurement of profit. Such measurement in the business world is certainly complex, but subject to detailed and strictly enforced accounting practices to ensure that businesses calculate profit in essentially the same way. While there are a few areas in universities with such conventions (such as the calculation of how much funded research a university conducts), the consensus on how to measure elements of university performance and the consequences of violating the agreements that do exist are much weaker than in the private sector.

Ranking academic institutions is an attempt to reduce the complexity and ambiguity of academic performance to a single number. Rankings are consulted by prospective students, their parents, and alumni. For this reason, academic leaders pay rankings a great deal of attention and strive to make theirs better. *U.S. News & World Report*'s rankings are the most influential for undergraduate institutions, but there are many others.[5] Rankings, like colleges and universities themselves, have increasingly become international and bring some discipline to the performance claims of academic organizations. (An old joke in business schools is that, prior to published rankings, there were fifty schools in the top ten.) And rankings sometimes are used imaginatively by colleges to show how strong they are compared with their competitors (such as "#1 among public liberal arts colleges in the Mid-Atlantic").

But the promise of rankings to find simplicity beyond the complexity of academic performance is a mirage. Here is why:

1. Publications that rank institutions need to choose from among many elements of college and university performance. If they choose only a few factors, the ranking is necessarily

an incomplete representation of the overall quality of the institution. If they choose many, the ranking requires a complex formula whose weights appear arbitrary and probably do not reflect the needs of any specific individual considering a school or college.

2. Whichever elements of performance are incorporated in the rankings, they must be measured, and the measure must be standardized across a wide range of institutions. The choice of measures has a significant and poorly understood impact on the final ranking. For example, think about how to assess the quality of the undergraduate student body. Consider high school grades and test scores? Entrepreneurial potential? Diversity? Character?

3. For many rankings (including those in *U.S. News & World Report*), a significant component of the formula is created simply by asking people (deans, provosts, presidents) to rate the quality of the institutions being ranked. We have done this ourselves, and the rankings questionnaires include hundreds of institutions, most of which we knew nothing about. This methodology introduces a deeply conservative bias into the rankings and further reinforces the "rich get richer" element of academic performance. Institutions with strong reputations continue to get high rankings of quality simply because of their reputations.

4. In many categories of universities and schools, there are only small differences in performance on measures of various goals. But the use of ordinal scores (literally, rankings) creates the illusion of much greater differences. Four colleges that score 9.75, 9.72, 9.68, and 9.62 on a composite measure that ranges from 1 to 10 will be ranked #1, #2, #3, and #4. (And in some cases, the raw scores are not even made public.) In this way, nuance and accuracy are traded for simplicity and the illusion of clear differences.

5. Colleges and universities simply do not change a great deal from one year to the next. But if the rankings stayed largely the same year after year, the public would lose interest. To combat this danger, rankers periodically update their formulas, leading to movement in the rankings. The extent to which this movement tracks actual changes in quality is anyone's guess.

6. Finally, and there is no nice way to say this, universities sometimes cheat. Cheating ranges from clever ways of calculating a measure (such as accepting students on a conditional basis so their SAT scores aren't included in the average, or hiring one's own students so they can be reported as employed post-graduation) to outright falsification of data.[6] In an attempt to discourage cheating, the rankings organizations provide instructions that look a lot like the tax code and require a senior executive to sign off, like the Sarbanes-Oxley requirement for public companies.[7]

Before we go on to discuss other differences between businesses and universities, it is worth pointing out a final difference in the relationship between profit and reputation (prestige, quality). Businesses of course care about their reputations and go to some lengths to measure and manage them. But reputation is cultivated as a means to long-term profitability and is subordinated to the need to be profitable. In contrast, universities strive to at least break even and sometimes have a small profit (although that is a term you will never see in their financial reports) at the end of the fiscal year. This profit is immediately invested in something intended to enhance the reputation of the college or university. So while reputation is a means to an end (of profit) in business, profit is a means to an end (of reputation) in academics. Dr. Patricia Beeson, professor of economics and provost emeritus at the University of Pittsburgh, takes this point one step further, explaining, "One could argue that universities are motivated by our ability and opportunity to advance and disseminate knowledge, and rankings and prestige are imperfect measures of any institution's ability to do so. Thus, one might say that profit is a means to an end (of advancing knowledge) in academics."[8]

CHAIN OF COMMAND

In business, a clear chain of command proceeds from the board of directors, to the CEO, to his or her direct reports, and then down and throughout the organization to the lowest level. This means that, within broad limits, someone more senior can direct someone more junior to do something, with the expectation that that person will in fact do it. If such a junior employee does not, that employee is putting his or her performance evaluation, and possibly job, in jeopardy. Organizations vary in how explicit they are about this fact. While some businesses try to soften it by using words like "teamwork" and "community," the chain of command is still fundamental to how they operate. As a consultant friend recently told us, "If the CEO says we are going to do something, we can discuss it, but we all know we are going to do it."

While there is a chain of command in academics, it is much less definitive than in most businesses. The closest universities come to a business-style chain of command is the relationship between the president and his or her direct reports, who work together in a way not particularly different from those in business. (And, as in business, wise presidents do not simply give orders without consultation and discussion.) University boards seldom order presidents to take a specific action, and when they do, it is generally a sign of trouble. And while presidents and provosts establish policies and budgets that constrain the actions of deans, it is rare for either to give anything like an order to deans, who enjoy considerable autonomy in leading their schools. This softness of command cascades down the ranks, as department heads have wide latitude in how they lead their departments and individual faculty have considerable discretion in how they conduct their teaching and research.

We will discuss the nature of organization and influence in universities in much more detail in chapters 5 and 6, including the concepts of academic freedom, free inquiry, and shared governance. For now, we will conclude by saying that anyone anticipating a business-style chain of command in an academic organization is likely to be disappointed. This is not hypothetical: we have seen deans who come from business wondering why no one did anything when they issued what would be perceived in a corporate setting as a direct order.

SENSE OF URGENCY

Business is known for its focus on the immediate future. The stereotypical businessperson is hurrying, trying to get a number of things done at once, asking subordinates to do things faster, and telling people that "time is money."[9] While this is to some degree a caricature, businesspeople are indeed focused on producing results, now. Business school students are taught that clarity and conciseness are key criteria of effective business communication. The concepts of discounted cash flow and net present value teach us that the timing of financial returns matters, and sooner is better. Customers who are not contacted right away may become someone else's customers. Deals that are not closed quickly may never happen.[10]

This is particularly true in publicly owned companies, where quarterly profits are dissected relative to their competitors, previous quarters, signals from the chief financial officer, and so on. This environment has created a constant sense of urgency in many businesspeople, as well as an industry devoted to addressing stress, work-life balance, and burnout.

While some aspects of academe are very much "on the clock," such as turning in grades or submitting grant proposals, most colleges and universities do not operate with the same short-term focus and sense of urgency as business. No doubt this is related to our discussion above about the absence of consensus on goals. Many high-level goals (for example, the quality of the incoming class or the percentage of graduates who find jobs) can be measured only annually. And many elements of university work, especially research, simply take a long time. As we will discuss in chapter 5, it can take five years or more in a PhD program to become a professor.

Another way to understand this gap in perspectives between the worlds of business and academics is to consider the rates of failure in the two sectors: business failure is routine, while university failure is very unusual. As Robert M. Hendrickson and his colleagues point out, "None of the original 30 industries listed on the Dow Jones Industrial Average in 1928 are on the list today, and many no longer exist at all, yet all 30 of the top universities in the country in 1928 still exist, and most of them would still be considered among the best."[11] At the other end of the scale, a recent study of "invisible colleges" (small, private, nonselective colleges) found that in the forty years between 1972 and 2012, only 16 percent of these potentially fragile institutions closed.[12]

When the president of Sweet Briar College in Virginia announced in 2015 that it was going to close due to serious financial problems, the event was breathlessly covered by the higher education press and even the national media.[13] In the end, however, Sweet Briar remained open. Consider this: even a college whose president wanted it to close didn't close. In summary, businesspeople live with the real existential threat that their business may fail, and many do. This fear simply does not exist in the vast majority of academic organizations.

The sense of urgency issue sometimes comes to a head in the context of faculty meetings. While the optimal business meeting follows a preset agenda, stays on time, and concludes with crisply made decisions, faculty meetings follow a somewhat different logic. As James G. March and Johan P. Olsen observed of academic organizations, decision-making is a stage for many dramas.[14] Meetings are remembered as much for a particularly eloquent argument as for the decision that was made (or not made). A dean we know who was fresh from a fairly buttoned-up corporation introduced a proposal at a faculty meeting, expecting quick acceptance so that they could move on to the next topic. As the faculty warmed to a discussion of the merits of and problems with the idea, the new dean asked someone what they were doing. He was told they were discussing the idea. "I'll be in my office," he said. "Let me know when they're finished."

AFFILIATION AND LOYALTY

Businesspeople's primary affiliation and loyalty is to the organization that employs them. If you ask them what they do, the company they work for will generally be part of the answer, and may even be the whole answer: "I work for IBM." This is not to say that businesspeople do not change employers; of course they do. And it is not to say that they are blindly loyal; of course they are not. But while they are working for a firm, their primary affiliation and loyalty is expected to be to that firm. Violating that expectation by doing something that materially helps a competitor would be a serious offense and could easily lead to termination.

In academic organizations, faculty have dual loyalties. While they are to varying degrees loyal to the institution that employs them (with the same limitations as above), faculty have another powerful allegiance, which is to their field. Faculty members affiliate very strongly with their academic area, or discipline, and while their interests often evolve during their academic career, actually changing from one field to another is quite rare. If you ask academics what they do, they may or may not mention the institution that employs them, but they will certainly say, "I am a philosopher" or "I teach chemistry."

There are a number of reasons for this divided allegiance. One is the existence of the "academic community," sometimes called the "invisible college." Faculty members who are employed by several different colleges over the course of their careers will nevertheless interact consistently with many of the same colleagues, regardless of who is paying any of them. This affiliation is reinforced by the existence of international professional organizations such as the Modern Language Association and the Academy of Management. Such associations meet at least annually, and the ties among academics at different institutions are regularly strengthened.[15]

Not just faculty affiliate closely with professional organizations. Most university administrators and staff members belong to national or international organizations associated with their functional unit; many attend national and regional conferences, hold leadership positions in these organizations, and find employment via the formal and informal professional networks provided by associations. Additionally, members of college administration organizations vote on nationally agreed-upon professional codes of conduct and ethics. Examples of these influential organizations include the National Association of Student Financial Aid Administrators (NASFAA), the Association of College and University Housing Officers (ACUHO), the National Association of Student Personnel Administrators (NASPA), and the National Association of Colleges and Employers (NACE). These organizations often operate on a national, regional, and statewide scale, such as the American Association of Collegiate Registrars and Admissions Officers (AACRAO), the Southern Association of Collegiate Registrars and Admissions Officers (SACRAO) and the Carolinas Association of Collegiate Registrars and Admissions Officers (CACRAO). Businesses affiliated with the higher education enterprise often also closely affiliate with these organizations.

Each academic field has a set of journals (discussed in detail in chapter 7), some of which are operated by the professional associations. The enterprise of creating, reviewing, and publishing research is connected to the field, not to the employing organization.[16] Faculty review potential articles for journals, and some take on the role of associate editor or editor, all on behalf of their discipline and only indirectly for their institution. Of course, businesspeople take voluntary positions in trade associations, but there is little doubt that the benefit of this work is expected to accrue primarily to their employer.

For most faculty, professors at other institutions play an important role in decisions about their career through the promotion and tenure process (see chapter 5). So faculty must have a focus on their discipline, not just on their institution, to be successful. They have to make sure that their work is known and respected by key people in their discipline. In the absence of all other factors, a focus on their field instead of on their institution would simply (and ironically) be a reasonable response to the incentives provided by their own institution.

Faculty simply see themselves as professionals in their discipline first and as employees of their university second. In fact, many faculty do not even consider themselves employees.[17] They believe deeply in the transcendent importance of their work, and the fact that it takes place in a particular physical location and is to some degree funded by a particular institution is secondary. Of course, many research faculty are funded largely by sources outside the institution (see chapter 7), which further complicates the question of loyalty.

For all of these reasons, businesspeople who join the academic world are likely to be surprised, even shocked, by the affiliation of many faculty.

THE NATURE OF WORK AND THE GUARANTOR OF QUALITY

Another significant difference between businesses and universities derives from the nature of the work that faculty perform and from their professional status. Much of the work in business is well understood, and processes have been created to govern how it is to be done. The stereotypical example, now mostly outmoded, is of course the assembly line, where absolute adherence to a process designed by industrial engineers is required of all employees. In the transition to a service economy, this philosophy has not been lost, as anyone who has called a technology company helpline has learned: "Please unplug your device, wait twenty seconds . . ." And as business and health care have converged, even the work of physicians is increasingly governed by clinical pathways, which are an attempt to improve medical outcomes through standardization of care and practice.

While of course there are differences among business functions (accounting is more routinized than marketing) and hierarchical levels (the bottom of the organization is more routinized than the top), in many areas of business someone has determined the best way to do something, and that generally is the way it is done. High quality and low cost are guaranteed by adherence to processes that have been worked out in advance.

Conversely, academic work is inherently hard to direct from above, if indeed there is any "above" in academics. Especially in research, faculty often do things that no one has done before and would be very difficult to routinize. The research enterprise depends on the creativity, innovation, and insights of faculty researchers, who have arrived at their positions for the very reason that they possess these characteristics.[18] Moreover, the opportunity to direct their own work is one of the main reasons faculty are attracted to their roles, and threats to academic freedom — real or perceived — are taken very seriously.[19]

In teaching as well, the evolution of knowledge and pedagogy (ways of teaching and learning) and the differences among students make it difficult to enforce the levels of standardization often found in business. Faculty, especially the best faculty, are always coming up with new approaches, new materials, and new tools and making mid-course adjustments to ensure that their students learn the material. Howard Aldrich and Solvi Lillejord refer to this approach as the "logic of discovery."[20] Faculty take pride in all of this, as well they should, as these practices positively impact their reputation in their particular field and the reputation of the institution that they represent.

Research and teaching take place in business as well as in academics. And both are more routinized in the former than in the latter. One of our friends who founded a training company said that he could tell what his trainers were doing on any given day practically down to the minute. Virtually no dean or department head would make this claim about what his or her faculty were teaching on a daily basis.[21] It cannot be the nature of the work alone that drives the differing levels of standardization in business and academics.

One reason for the lack of standardization in academic organizations is the low degree of interdependence among units. As Hendrickson and his colleagues put it, "In most colleges and universities, academic affairs is a confederation of loosely aligned academic departments that have minimal interaction with each other, and decisions by department heads have little impact on other units."[22] In this environment, there is less need for standardization than in the average business, where it is used, among other purposes, to coordinate the interdependence among units. Professional schools (law, business, medicine) are often an exception to this rule: they have a more integrated approach to the curriculum and higher expectations of consistent coverage of certain material.

Finally, academics fervently believe that it is their professionalism — their standards, skills, experience, and judgment — that guarantees quality and high academic performance; this is an article of faith among professors, which they share with other disciplines (or guilds, to use John Lombardi's term).[23] As Jerry Muller explains, "[This] professional ethos is based on mastery of a specialized knowledge acquired through an extended process of education and training; autonomy and control over work; an identification with one's group and a sense of responsibility toward colleagues; a high valuation of intrinsic rewards; and a commitment to the interests of clients above considerations of cost."[24] With the exception of the part about clients, this captures perfectly the worldview of most academics.

The public counts on engineers to ensure the structural integrity of buildings, on attorneys to provide sound legal judgment, and on accountants to expertly judge the quality of a firm's financial statements. Academics expect no less deference in their decisions about teaching and research. Directives from above generally are perceived as unnecessary and disruptive incursions from people who do not have expertise in their field and likely will lead to lower quality faculty performance. In general, belief in the importance of faculty professionalism is enshrined in the culture of academic institutions through the concept of academic freedom (see chapter 5).

ATTITUDES ABOUT GROWTH

A final striking difference between business and academics concerns growth. In a nutshell, businesses are for it, and academics are against it. Growth is a signal of a thriving business, whose potential for profit increases with its size. Leadership in revenues and market share is a common area for competition among businesses in an industry.[25] How much and how fast to grow is often a key component of business strategy.

Businesspeople often are surprised at the lack of interest in growth, at least as measured by number of students, among academic organizations. But the reason for this difference should be clear from our earlier discussion of profit versus prestige. While the former likely increases at larger scale, the latter likely decreases. If student selectivity is an indicator of prestige (and it is often a component of rankings), then growth in enrollment runs the risk of decreasing selectivity. Lombardi has an interesting analysis of this in which he concludes that a university with one great teacher and one great student may be the reductio ad absurdum of this line of thinking.[26] In a series of many conversations we recently had with faculty about academic performance indicators, not a single one even mentioned growth or size.

UNIVERSITY
- Many differing goals
- Limited authority
- Long time frame for decisions
- Mixed allegiances
- Professionalization
- Limited interest in growth

BUSINESS
- Profit goal
- Clear chain of command
- Short time frame for decisions
- Clear allegiance to the organization
- Standardization
- Desire for growth

1.2. Differences between universities and businesses.

Interestingly, some universities have rejected the principle that small is beautiful and have intentionally grown very large, including Arizona State University (more than 70,000 students) and the University of Central Florida (more than 60,000). Arizona State president Michael Crow has argued that this kind of growth represents the future of universities, but this argument is heresy to many if not most academics.[27]

How Are Businesses and Universities Similar?

BUSINESS OPERATIONS

While we have emphasized the core activities of teaching and research in colleges, these institutions, of course, do much more, and many of the other things they do also are done by businesses, such as these:

- They communicate their value to potential students.
- They communicate their value to potential donors and legislators.
- They make tuition decisions.
- They maintain the campus.
- They operate dormitories and cafeterias.
- They ensure the financial solvency of the institution.

This list makes it clear that many activities undertaken by universities are nearly identical to the activities of businesses. As we will discuss further in chapter 9, these activities provide ample opportunities for businesspeople to use their accumulated knowledge, expertise, and experience to assist colleges and universities.

THE WAR FOR TALENT

The term "war for talent" became popular about twenty years ago and indicates that organizational success depends on the ability to attract, develop, and retain talented people, who are scarce relative to the needs of business.[28] The field of talent management grew out of human resources in recognition of this basic organizational understanding. Its tenets include that the most talented people have a disproportionate impact on the success of their organization and that they will leave if they are unhappy. Ed Michaels, Helen Handfield-Jones, and Beth Axelrod focus primarily on managerial talent: "people who can lead a company, division, or function; guide a new product team; supervise a shift in an industrial plant; or manage a store with 15 or 150 associates." While some business leaders have learned from this only to mouth the bromide "People are our most important asset," talent management is taken seriously in a large and growing set of business organizations.[29]

The war for talent is as important if not more in academic institutions, whose reputations are disproportionately built on the accomplishments of a small number of faculty. When Nobel Prize winners are announced, even the most prestigious universities lavish a great deal of attention on the new laureates (famously, guaranteed free parking!), who represent far less than 1 percent of their faculty. Many universities use distinguished professorships to recognize, reward, and retain their best faculty (see chapter 5).

The closeness of the international academic community guarantees that the field as a whole knows who are the best performers, where they are employed, and whether they are "movable." It is not uncommon for a distinguished faculty member who is seen as movable to have several job offers at once. These offers can be initiated very quietly simply through invitations for professors to give research seminars at other institutions. Once a prominent faculty member is in play, however, the situation can quickly become a feeding frenzy. It is hard to think of examples of this in business, as the communication among executives in an industry cannot hold a candle to that among professors in a discipline.

In the provost's office at the University of North Carolina, one of our key responsibilities was faculty retention. If a faculty member had an outside offer (and sometimes if he or she did not, yet), we would see if we could offer better compensation, perhaps better research support—whatever it took to keep that person. In this way we were able to retain the majority of faculty who were being recruited to leave, but the process was arduous and expensive.

Before leaving this topic, we should point out that the war for talent encompasses "rookie" faculty. Hiring new faculty is often a two-step process that begins with a number of brief interviews at professional meetings and then moves, for the short list, to one- to two-day interviews on campus. During these interviews, candidates will give a talk based on their research and meet people connected to the hiring department. An extraordinary amount of institutional resources is devoted to the assessment and recruitment of these faculty candidates, in hopes of attracting the discipline's next stars. We discuss this process in greater detail in chapter 5.

DIVERSE STAKEHOLDER EXPECTATIONS

Stakeholder expectations could be seen as either a similarity or a difference. The diversity of stakeholder expectations is familiar to business leaders. In public companies, shareholders (the original stakeholders) want growing share prices or profits that are returned to them via dividends. The occurrence of shareholders loudly making demands along these lines at shareholder meetings is increasingly common, which actually makes businesses *more* like universities. Employees want high wages, a desire that has a complicated relationship with profitability, as well as stable employment. Customers want high-quality products and services at low prices. Communities in which the firm operates want good corporate citizenship (for example, corporate engagement, contributions to local charities) and collaboration on issues of mutual concern (such as environmental impact). Government entities insist on regulatory compliance.

Colleges and universities also have many stakeholders and concerns. Boards and legislators for public universities want to see efficient operations that make the best use of tax dollars. Faculty and staff want high wages and stable employment. Faculty want investment in their research and teaching. Students and their parents want an excellent education, low tuition and fees, and employment after graduation. Communities want good university citizenship (such as academic support for addressing local problems) and collaboration on issues of mutual concern (for example, parking, public transportation, student housing, and conduct). Government entities insist on regulatory compliance. In 1958, University of California president Clark Kerr provided a now-famous description of university stakeholders: "The three major administrative problems on a campus are sex for the students, athletics for the alumni, and parking for the faculty."[30] Sixty years on, few would argue that much has changed.

Similar to most businesses, universities are surrounded by constituencies who want very different things from them—stakeholders who are not shy about expressing what they want. The difference, as discussed above, is the institutionalized primacy of shareholders and profit for businesses.[31] Businesses see the demands of other stakeholders through the lens of their own need to be profitable. Universities have no such luxury, and any of their constituencies can make life miserable for them, with no ability to defend decisions in terms of one transcendent goal.

MULTIFACETED COMPETITION

Competition could also be seen as a similarity or a difference, but it is more of a similarity than most businesspeople understand it to be. It is axiomatic that businesses experience competition, particularly in the area of sales but also in hiring talented employees, as we discussed above. Colleges and universities and their faculty likewise compete in a variety of ways, including competition for

- the best faculty;
- the best students;
- reputation/prestige/quality/rankings;[32]
- membership in honorary societies, such as the National Academies;
- research funding via grants and contracts (see chapter 7);
- donor support; and
- publications in top journals.

While it may not appear so from the outside, colleges and universities actually operate in extremely competitive environments. The exact nature of the competition (such as for students as opposed to grants) is different for different types of academic institutions (see chapter 2) but is significant in virtually every kind of college or university. This is especially the case when resources (grant dollars, state funding, number of students graduating from high school) are decreasing.

Anyone who has sent a child to college is aware of the lengths to which universities go to compete for the best students. Universities buy lists of students who score high on entrance exams, create elaborate interactive websites, strive to find the newest innovations in campus tours, and use complex models to determine how much financial aid they need to offer each student, not to mention the now-clichéd gourmet cafeterias, lazy rivers, and yes, rock-climbing walls, which we are pretty sure was a meme before the word was invented.

Competition for donor largesse is similarly intense. When I (JD) was involved in fund-raising as a business school dean, donors would typically have a half-dozen nonprofit organizations among which they allocated their contributions. Often two or three universities would be on the list, not to mention their children's private schools, which somehow managed to enforce the principle that contributions were not voluntary without actually calling them tuition. I was always impressed by this trick, but it made the competition for philanthropic dollars even tougher.

LIMITED RESOURCES AND THE NEED FOR STRATEGIC PRIORITIES

A final similarity between businesses and universities—and for that matter virtually all organizations—is the condition of limited resources. At any given time, there are more demands than there are funds. The severity of this issue ebbs and flows with the economy and with organizations' performance. But any number of initiatives and projects are always waiting to be funded and people are always ready to advocate for each of them. In order to address budget decision-making, both businesses and universities employ budgeting systems informed by a set of priorities, which in the best case are connected to the organization's strategy.

The similarity ends, however, when businesses use the goal of profitability to decide among competing uses of funds. Investments may be seen as cutting operating costs, better serving customers, or improving the quality of life for employees (and any of these may be strategic priorities), but they must connect in some way back to the business's primary goal of profit. The ensuing analysis generally involves some type of return-on-investment calculation, in which the amount of the in-

UNIVERSITY   BUSINESS

Business operations
War for talent
Diverse stakeholder expectations
Multifaceted competition
Limited resources and the need for strategic priorities

1.3. Similarities between universities and businesses.

vestment is tested against its ability to enhance revenues or decrease costs.

Since universities have no such bottom line, it is more difficult to decide among potential institutional investments. Those making the case for investments under conditions of scarcity need to argue both for the importance of the goal they are pursuing and how their idea will help to accomplish the goal. The institution's mission is often invoked in these discussions—for example, "The education of undergraduates is among our core functions, and investment in classroom technology will help us meet our pedagogical needs." Interestingly, rankings, the most obvious proxy for a bottom line, are seldom mentioned in these discussions, perhaps because the tenuous validity of the rankings is all too familiar, both to those making the arguments and to those making the decisions.

One of our interviewees has been both a CEO and a university board chair. He recalled that his university presented a plan to the board that had more than fifty priorities. Perhaps speaking for businesspeople everywhere, he said, "That's not a strategy; that's a wish list."

What Kinds of Businesses Are Most Like Universities?

We find universities to be most like professional service firms, such as consulting firms, law firms, and public accounting firms, and our friends in these organizations to be somewhat professorial. Businesspeople coming from such organizations—especially strategy consulting firms—should experience less culture shock than those who engage with higher education from other types of businesses.

All of these types of firms are run by professionals, and maintaining professional standards is critically important to the success of their organizations.[33] While there certainly are policies and rules as in other businesses, professional service firms rely heavily on the professional judgment of their consultants, attorneys, or auditors. These individuals have a great deal of power in their respective organizations. Also like universities, these firms place top priority on their professional reputations, as reputation helps them to attract and recruit talented university and professional school graduates as employees. These firms also engage heavily in research and thought leadership, publishing articles that inform practice.

The idea of colleagueship is also common to both professional service firms and universities. Fellow professionals are not just employees who happen to work at the same firm; they share a professional bond and identity, and they realize that the reputation of the firm is dependent on each of them. Finally, the professionals in these firms are backed up by a significant staff of people who support their work, although developments in information technology have led to less staff support in both universities and professional service firms.

One important difference between professional service firms and academic institutions is the existence in the former of customers whose needs must be consistently met. While it may be clear to businesspeople that students are the "customers" of colleges and universities, this equivalence is not accepted by most academics, who see it as commercializing and diminishing the relationship between faculty and students and as further evidence of the unfortunate trend toward the corporatization of higher education.

In summary, while universities have many elements that resemble businesses, the differences are such that it is misguided to try to turn a college or university into a business. American colleges and universities are revered for their contributions to our democracy, and their longevity is to be applauded. This is not to say that some business practices should not be applied to universities; indeed, they should—for example, consistent and strategically driven budget models and competitive recruiting and retention of talented people.

2

American Colleges and Universities

So far, we have discussed academic organizations as if they were all alike. In this chapter, we will explore the many varieties of colleges and universities in the United States and how they are similar and different. We focus in this book on four-year nonprofit institutions, but several other kinds of institutions exist in American higher education,[1] and they play important roles. Table 2.1 shows the number of institutions of different types that are found in the United States and how many students are enrolled in each type.[2]

Before we focus on four-year nonprofit institutions, several points about the bigger picture seem worthwhile. First, despite the rise of for-profit institutions in the United States, the majority of students in either two-year or four-year institutions are enrolled in the nonprofit segment of higher education. Second, there are relatively few private two-year institutions; this sector is dominated by public institutions. Third, these public two-year institutions serve a great number of students. When thinking about the American system of higher education, it is important to keep in mind the critical role of community colleges and other two-year institutions.

Public and Private Institutions

Among four-year nonprofits, the distinction between public and private institutions is among the most profound. Public universities are owned, operated, and funded with few exceptions by states, whereas

Table 2.1. Different Types of Higher Education Institutions in the United States and Their Total Enrollment (2015)

	Institutions		Fall 2014 Enrollment	
	Number	% of Total	Number	% of Total
Doctoral universities	335	7	6,455,622	32
Master's colleges and universities	741	16	4,422,535	22
Baccalaureate colleges	583	13	999,834	5
Baccalaureate/associate's	408	9	1,079,576	5
Associate's colleges	1,113	24	6,524,819	32
Special focus: two-year	444	10	204,321	1
Special focus: four-year	1,005	22	776,979	4
Tribal colleges	35	1	17,929	0.1
Total	4,664		20,481,615	

Source: Carnegie Classification database, Facts and Figures 2015, accessed May 12, 2018, http://carnegieclassifications.iu.edu/downloads/CCIHE2015-FactsFigures.pdf.

private universities are privately owned (most often by nonprofit corporations), operated, and funded. Boards of public universities are responsible to their state governments for their handling of these institutions, while private university boards operate more independently.

Both public and private institutions of higher education have deep roots in America. Harvard and Yale are the oldest private universities, with charters dating to the seventeenth and early eighteenth centuries, making them both much older than the country itself. Among public universities, the University of Georgia, the University of North Carolina at Chapel Hill, and the College of William & Mary originated in the seventeenth and eighteenth centuries.[3] The growth of public universities was given a major shot in the arm by the Morrill Act of 1862, establishing land-grant universities, which number over 100 today. These institutions originally focused on agriculture, science and engineering, and military science, but today their portfolio is much more comprehensive.[4]

MISSION

Public and private universities have overlapping missions: both are dedicated to education, research, and service. But the missions of public universities are usually weighted toward the state in which they are located[5] and which has historically supported them through taxpayer funding, particularly as applied to the teaching and service missions of these institutions. Public universities disproportionately educate residents of their state, especially at the undergraduate level, which means that public universities are often less selective in admissions than private universities.[6] Many public universities also engage in research and public service projects to benefit their respective states.

The mission statement of UNC–Chapel Hill illustrates this focus and also captures the balancing act of leading public universities between their responsibility to their state and to the broader good:

> The University of North Carolina at Chapel Hill, the nation's first public university, serves North Carolina, the United States, and the world through teaching, research, and public service. We embrace an unwavering commitment to excellence as one of the world's great research universities. Our mission is to serve as a center for research, scholarship, and creativity and to teach a diverse community of undergraduate, graduate, and professional students to become the next generation of leaders. Through the efforts of our exceptional faculty and staff, and with generous support from North Carolina's citizens, we invest our knowledge and resources to enhance access to learning and to foster the success and prosperity of each rising generation.[7]

Notable former UNC president William Friday made the connection between the university and the state more personal in his advice to students: "Every morning a million North Carolinians get up and go to work for wages which leave them below the poverty line so they can pay taxes that finance the education you receive at Carolina. Your job is to figure out how you're going to pay them back."[8] In fairness to the citizens of North Carolina, the state is much more successful economically now than it was when this statement was made.

SIZE

While there are more private than public colleges and universities in the United States, the latter enroll many more students, on average three to four times more. This size difference is skewed by the truly giant universities, all of which are public. The ten largest universities, which are located in Arizona, Florida, Indiana, Michigan, Minnesota,

Ohio, and Texas, collectively enroll more than 500,000 students.[9] This discrepancy in size is a fundamental difference between public and private institutions and is most likely due to their respective missions. Public universities were created to serve the public, whereas private institutions can serve whomever they wish. A few private institutions have gone against the grain: for example, Brigham Young University and New York University each enroll more than 30,000 students.[10]

WEALTH

University endowments are funds invested by the institution for the long term. Universities annually spend a small portion of their endowment (usually 4 to 6 percent) to support operations, the goal being to spend at a level to preserve, if not grow, the value of the endowment. Endowments provide some stability in funding from year to year and often are used for student aid, faculty salaries, and libraries.[11] Differences in wealth between public and private universities are the inverse of the differences in size: the wealthiest universities are most often private. Four of the five largest endowments in the United States belong to private universities, seven of the top ten, and fifteen of the top twenty. The endowments of Harvard, Yale, Stanford, Princeton, MIT, Penn, and Columbia collectively represent well over $100 billion, or roughly 25 percent of all university endowments.[12]

If we analyze wealth and size together, the differences are even more striking, as the ten institutions with the largest endowments, in excess of $1 million per student and in a few cases over $2 million, are all private.[13] One might suspect that these universities could cover the costs of educating students indefinitely without charging tuition. But much of these funds are restricted, via donor agreements, for other specific purposes. And most private universities have *much* smaller endowments: their median endowment was about $7.9 million in 2014.[14] Wealth in private universities is analogous to size in publics; the overall picture is skewed by a few very wealthy institutions.[15]

STATE SUPPORT

Of course, one reason private universities require large endowments is that by definition they do not receive state support. Over the past twenty-five years, public support for public colleges and universities has ranged from a low of about $6,000 per student to a high of about $10,000 per student in 2016 dollars.[16] State support peaked in 2001, with significant decreases after 2008 and some recovery in the past few years. If we take $8,000 to be a typical annual level of support per student, it is equivalent for public universities to an endowment of about $160,000 per student (based on a 5 percent annual draw on the endowment). As the average public four-year university has about 13,000 students, this equates to an endowment of roughly $2 billion. Nevertheless, as public support for public higher education has waned, universities have looked elsewhere (such as to grants, tuition, out-of-state students, and philanthropy) for funding, giving rise to the term PINO, or "public in name only."

TUITION AND FEES

Private universities charge their students much higher tuition, which also can be seen as offsetting the absence of state support. The average total tuition and fees at private universities for undergraduates in 2017–18 was about $35,000, while for resident (in-state) students at public universities the comparable figure was about $10,000. This lower tuition is seen as reflecting both the subsidies offered by the state and the commitment to access that has long been the hallmark of American public higher education. Public universities charged nonresident students, however, about $26,000 in tuition and fees.[17] Many public universities have increased nonresident enrollment to offset cuts in state support, which has earned them considerable criticism for moving away from their historical mission.[18] Robert A. Scott concisely summarizes these developments in state support and tuition, and board members of public institutions should take note: "Since 2008, state funding for public universities has been cut by 28 percent, while tuition has increased an average of 27 percent."[19]

Board members also need to be aware of tuition discounting, an institutional strategy to attract enrolling students. Many universities provide a discount on their published tuition and fees (or "sticker price") by providing aid in grants to students and their families based on what they are able to pay. "[An institution's] discount rate represents the portion of total tuition and fee revenue channeled back to students as grant-based financial aid," explains Marjorie Valbrun in *Inside Higher Ed*.[20] Many universities have a discount rate above 40 percent, which can be a risky financial strategy. "With growing discount rates, colleges undercut their bottom line and slowed the growth of net tuition revenue," Valbrun reported, citing a 2017 annual report by the National Association of College and University Business Officers.[21] Boards need to know their institution's discount rate and how it affects tuition and fee revenues. According to a brief issued by the Association of Governing Boards, "Some colleges rely so heavily on discounting that when they raise their tuition, they do not generate new net revenues. In today's economic climate, where students and families are struggling financially, some institutions are so afraid of losing students to lower-priced institutions that they are discounting away their needed operating revenues. That is not a viable long-term strategy, and it threatens an institution's ability to offer the educational opportunities that allow it to fulfill its mission."[22] We discuss college and university finances further in chapter 8.

PRESTIGE AND RANKINGS

In chapter 1 we discussed reputation and prestige as the closest thing to a bottom line for academic institutions and rankings as a popular if imperfect way to measure these ineffable qualities. At the highest end of the prestige scale, there is no contest between public and private universities, as reflected in the "National Universities Ranking" section of the *U.S. News & World Report*: the top twenty universities are all private. More broadly, twenty-three of the top twenty-five and thirty-seven of the top fifty national universities are private. Beyond that, the dominance of the private schools weakens, as only fifty-four of the top hundred national universities are private and forty-six are public.[23]

There is likely an implicit belief among both providers and consumers of higher education that, all things being equal, private institutions are more prestigious than public institutions. Beyond this, however, the prominence of private universities is to some degree predicated on the *U.S. News & World Report* rankings methodology, which includes graduation and retention rates (which are higher for more selective private colleges), perceived quality by academic leaders (see discussion in chapter 1), faculty salaries (generally higher in private schools), student selectivity, and so on.[24] In other words, the rankings are based on the values of private institutions, such as wealth and selectivity.

To address this perception of rankings, organizations have created alternative rankings based on different values. For example, the *New York Times* created the College Access Index, a measure of economic diversity more consistent with the values and missions of public universities. This index is based on the number of low-income students (Pell

Table 2.2. Number of Four-Year Nonprofit Institutions by Carnegie Classification and Institutional Control (Public or Private)

	Public	Private	Total
Doctoral universities	182	79	261
Doctoral/professional universities	31	114	145
Master's colleges and universities	254	289	543
Baccalaureate colleges	106	410	516
Total	573	892	1,465

Source: Carnegie Classification, accessed December 20, 2017, http://carnegieclassifications.iu.edu/.

Grant recipients) enrolled and how high the actual tuition paid is for middle-income students (lower is better). In this ranking, seven of the top ten institutions are public.[25] However, no one would mistake this ranking for an indication of prestige.

While both are bedrocks of American higher education, public and private colleges and universities are different in many ways. Private institutions enroll fewer students, are wealthier, receive no state support, and charge higher tuition. Public institutions enroll more students and specifically more in-state students, are less wealthy, receive important but dwindling state support, and charge lower tuition, especially to in-state students.

CARNEGIE CLASSIFICATION

Recognizing that there are important differences among academic institutions beyond public versus private, the Carnegie Commission on Higher Education instituted in 1970 (and has repeatedly updated) a classification system for American colleges and universities.[26] The Carnegie Classification divides four-year nonprofit institutions into three categories: doctoral universities, master's colleges and universities, and baccalaureate colleges. Table 2.2 shows the number of colleges and universities in each category, both public and private.[27]

Doctoral universities. This category "includes institutions that awarded at least 20 research/scholarship doctoral degrees during the [current] year."[28] Such institutions produce the PhDs who become university faculty (see chapter 5) and other professionals. This category is further subdivided into three subcategories—Very High Research Activity (R1), High Research Activity (R2), and Doctoral/Professional—

based on total research activity (conducting funded research and conferring doctoral degrees) and research activity per faculty member. In 2018 the Carnegie Classification was changed to include the Doctoral/Professional category and acknowledge institutions that confer more than thirty "professional practice" doctoral degrees in at least two programs. Greg Toppo in *Inside Higher Ed* points out that "so-called first professional degrees—which include the M.D., J.D., Pharm.D., D.Div. and others—hadn't previously been considered in the Carnegie listings."[29]

The public universities in the Very High Research category are generally the most prominent such institutions in the country or are flagship public universities (for example, the University of Michigan, the University of New Hampshire, and the University of California, Berkeley). Among the private institutions in this category are Ivy League institutions such as Princeton and Columbia but also prestigious universities from all over the country, including Chicago, Duke, Georgetown, and Stanford. Public universities in the High Research category include a few flagships (the University of Vermont, the University of Montana, and the University of Wyoming) and other prominent state universities. The private schools include such institutions as Catholic University and the University of Tulsa. The new category of Doctoral/Professional includes such public schools as Towson, Middle Tennessee State University, and Miami of Ohio and such private schools as Drake, Elon, Pepperdine, and the Mayo Clinic Graduate School of Biomedical Sciences.

Master's colleges and universities. This category "includes institutions that awarded at least 50 master's degrees and fewer than 20 doctoral degrees during the [current] year." There are many more of these institutions than there are doctoral universities. Private institutions are predominant in the master's category, which is subdivided into Larger (M1, over 200 degrees granted), Medium (M2, between 100 and 199 degrees granted), and Smaller (M3, between 50 and 99 degrees granted) designations. Larger master's universities include twelve universities in the California State University system and seven colleges in the City University of New York system, as well as other public universities such as Clarion in Pennsylvania and private schools such as Ithaca College in New York and Butler University in Indiana.

Medium master's schools include mostly private colleges and universities, most of which have a regional focus. A number of historically black colleges and universities are in this group, such as Winston-Salem

Table 2.3. Example Institutions in Each Classification

	Public	*Private*
Doctoral universities	University of North Carolina at Chapel Hill	Carnegie Mellon University
Doctoral/professional universities		Gonzaga University
Master's colleges and universities	University of Wisconsin– Eau Claire	
Baccalaureate colleges	United States Air Force Academy	Pomona College

State in North Carolina and Lincoln in Pennsylvania, as are a number of religious-affiliated schools, such as two Mount St. Mary's Universities (California and Maryland). Smaller master's colleges and universities are again mostly private, with a local or regional focus, and are similar to the previous group, only smaller.

Baccalaureate colleges. This final category includes "institutions where baccalaureate or higher degrees represent at least 50 percent of all degrees but where fewer than 50 master's degrees or 20 doctoral degrees were awarded during the [current] year."[30] This category represents nearly the same number of schools as the master's category and is more strongly dominated by private institutions. The two subcategories in the baccalaureate colleges group are the "institutions in which at least half of bachelor's degree majors in arts and sciences fields were included in the 'Arts & Sciences' group" and the institutions "included in the 'Diverse Fields' group."[31] These institutions are focused on undergraduate education.

This category includes a number of well-known liberal arts colleges (Bryn Mawr, Middlebury, Morehouse, Swarthmore), a number of religious-affiliated schools (St. Anselm, St. Johns, St. Michael's, and St. Vincent), and the five service academies. The other institutions in this category tend to be very small and focused on a particular geographical or career niche.

We have identified specific colleges or universities as examples of these categories in table 2.3. These examples will help us go beyond statistics and give the reader a sense of what schools are like in each category.

2.1. The Old Well on the University of North Carolina at Chapel Hill campus is among its most frequently visited locations and is featured in the university's logo. (University of North Carolina at Chapel Hill)

Public Universities

THE UNIVERSITY OF NORTH CAROLINA AT CHAPEL HILL

The University of North Carolina at Chapel Hill was founded in 1789 in the central part of the state. A nearby area is known as the Research Triangle, based on a research park that leverages the intellectual capital of the major universities in the area (including Duke University in Durham and North Carolina State University in Raleigh). The university's first student, Hinton James, famously walked 160 miles from Wilmington to enroll. (It is said that Hinton James Residence Hall honors him by being the farthest from the classrooms.) The state constitution declares that "the benefits of the University, as far as practicable, [should] be extended ... free of expense for tuition."

UNC certainly charges tuition, but it is among the lowest of leading public universities for resident students, in deference to this admonition. Only white men were originally admitted, but since the 1960s, admission has been open to all, and today's student body is quite diverse. Students and many North Carolina citizens are passionate about UNC sports, especially basketball. The Tar Heels nickname derives from a story about North Carolina soldiers sticking courageously to their place in battle (as if they had tar on their heels) and is related to the great pine forests of the state, which were the source of tar for boats. UNC today is a large, comprehensive research university; is among the most prominent public institutions in the United States; and attracts students from around the world. It has roughly $1 billion in research funding and nearly 30,000 students. Its schools of business, dentistry, medicine, pharmacy, and public health are world leaders. The Departments of Religious Studies and Sociology are among the very best. See table 2.4 for additional details on UNC.

THE UNIVERSITY OF WISCONSIN–EAU CLAIRE

The University of Wisconsin–Eau Claire was founded in 1916 as the Eau Claire State Normal School, preparing teachers and principals.[32] Classes took place in a single building in Eau Claire, a city in the Chippewa Valley in western Wisconsin. The university had several different names before adopting its current name in 1971. Even as a teacher's college, Eau Claire offered two years of general education. It began offering four-year bachelor's degrees in education in 1927 and in liberal arts in 1951. The institution became a university in the 1960s, adding schools of business and nursing. While Wisconsin–Eau Claire retains deep roots in western Wisconsin, its students take advantage of study-abroad programs in nearly thirty countries around the world. The university is home to an honors program and an award-winning jazz ensemble. Many students participate in high-impact learning experiences such as undergraduate research. The UW–Eau Claire Blugolds compete in NCAA Division III in twenty-two sports, including football and ice hockey. The university is an important source of pride in its region due to its academics, sports, and economic impact. See table 2.4 for additional details on Wisconsin–Eau Claire.

THE UNITED STATES AIR FORCE ACADEMY

The U.S. Air Force Academy was founded in 1954, seven years after the air force had become a separate service to train the country's future airmen.[33] It is the youngest of the five service academies. Once Congress authorized the academy, the air force considered potential sites all over the country, eventually deciding on Colorado Springs. The federal government purchased the necessary property, and the state of Colorado put up $1 million to facilitate the purchase (see below; prices had gone up since Gonzaga's $936 land deal). The first class, in 1955, was

2.2. University of Wisconsin–Eau Claire campus. (University of Wisconsin–Eau Claire)

2.3. The Cadet Chapel at the U.S. Air Force Academy.
(Trevor Cokley, United States Air Force)

sworn in at a temporary location, but the new site was ready in 1958 and the first class graduated from there in 1959.

The first women accepted to the academy enrolled in 1976 and graduated in 1980. The academy was declared a national historic landmark in 2004. The core curriculum includes STEM subjects and arts and humanities. It is oriented around nine institutional outcomes, some of which can be found at any institution (critical thinking, principles of science) while others are more air force–specific (national security, warrior ethos). The academy offers twenty-nine majors and several minors. Its athletics teams, the Fighting Falcons, compete in twenty-nine NCAA Division I sports in the Mountain West Conference. See table 2.4 for additional details on the U.S. Air Force Academy.

Private Universities

CARNEGIE MELLON UNIVERSITY

In 1900, Scottish immigrant Andrew Carnegie, who had become very wealthy in the steel business, founded a technical school in Pittsburgh; he envisioned it as a place where working-class men and women could learn applied engineering and design skills to build careers and communities. The school expanded to include baccalaureate degrees and became known as the Carnegie Institute of Technology in 1912. Graduate degrees were soon offered, and research became an important part of the institution's mission. The arts formed part of the curriculum from the beginning, and music and drama were added as important fields of study by 1914. Schools of business and public affairs, both committed to a quantitative analytic approach to these fields, were included by the mid-twentieth century. Carnegie Tech became Carnegie Mellon University in 1967 after a merger with the Mellon Institute, a scientific research center founded by the Mellon family. The university today is a highly ranked and highly selective institution. It has also become a major American and international power, with sites in Silicon Valley, New York, Australia, Portugal, Rwanda, and Qatar and students from over 100 countries. The university has developed world-class programs in business, computer science, engineering, data sciences, and information systems, among many others. It has been a leader in the development of information technology and artificial intelligence and of innovative applications in education, science, and national security. The university's Scottish roots are reflected in a number of traditions,

Table 2.4. Characteristics of Three Public Universities

	UNC–Chapel Hill	University of Wisconsin–Eau Claire	U.S. Air Force Academy
Governance and Carnegie Classification	Board of Trustees and N.C. System Board of Governors (R1)	Wisconsin Board of Regents (Master's)	Chief of staff of the Air Force and board of visitors (Baccalaureate)
Research funding*	$1,045,338,000	$1,238,000	$55 million
Number of schools/FT faculty†	13/3,887	4/449	1/500
Undergraduates/graduate students/total	18,523/10,946/29,469	9,981/648/10,629	4,237/0/4,237
Undergrad tuition resident/nonresident	$9,005/$34,588	$8,816/$16,736	NA/NA
Endowment/per student	$2.9 billion/$98,408	$56.1 million/$5,278	$60 million/$14,000
U.S. News ranking 2018	30th in National Universities	37th in Regional Universities Midwest	26th in National Liberal Arts Colleges
Acceptance rate (undergrad)	27%	89%	15%

*Rankings by total research and development expenditures, National Science Foundation; accessed December 21, 2017, https://ncsesdata.nsf.gov/profiles/site?method=rankingBySource&ds=herd.
† Numbers from respective university websites.

2.4. The Carnegie Mellon University campus. (Carnegie Mellon University)

including a bagpipe ensemble and a marching band whose members wear kilts. The school's "color" is the Carnegie clan's tartan. See table 2.5 for additional details on Carnegie Mellon.

GONZAGA UNIVERSITY

Gonzaga was founded in 1887 as Gonzaga College by Jesuit priest Fr. Joseph Cataldo, who had bought the property that would become the campus in 1881 with $936 in silver dollars.[34] The campus is in Spokane, Washington, in the northeastern part of the state. The school's original mission was to train priests, and the first class consisted of eighteen young men. Now called Gonzaga University, a coeducational institution, it offers both graduate (business, engineering, law) and undergraduate degrees in a diverse set of fields.[35] The Jesuit spirit of educating the whole person—mind, body, and spirit—informs the educational philosophy of the institution, whose motto is "Ad Majorem Dei Gloriam," or "For the greater glory of God." Students are taught by faculty in mostly small classes, as well as in online (graduate) programs. The university welcomes students of all faiths and has enrolled many international students; it is ranked highly among regional universities in the West. Gonzaga participates in the University of Washington School of Medicine's WWAMI program, an innovative regional initiative utiliz-

2.5. The Gonzaga University campus. (Gonzaga University)

2.6. The Pomona College campus. (Pomona College)

ing shared resources for medical education.[36] Gonzaga's athletic teams, known as the Bulldogs or Zags, compete in a number of sports in NCAA Division I. Bing Crosby and John Stockton (former NBA star) graduated from Gonzaga. See table 2.5 for additional details on Gonzaga.

POMONA COLLEGE

Pomona College, founded in 1887, is in Claremont, California, thirty-five miles east of Los Angeles. The college was founded by members of the Congregationalist faith who wanted to recreate a New England col-

Table 2.5. Characteristics of Three Private Universities

	Carnegie Mellon University	Gonzaga University	Pomona College
Governance and Carnegie Classification	Board of trustees (R1)	Board of trustees (doctoral/professional)	Board of trustees (baccalaureate)
Research funding*	$319,168,000	$959,000	$3.7 million
Number of schools/FT faculty†	7/1,391	6/441	1/188
Undergraduates/graduate students/total	6,673/7,288/13,961	5,160/2,407/7,567	1,660/0/1,660
Undergraduate tuition	$53,910	$37,990	$51,075
Endowment‡/per student	$1.3 billion/$93,116	$56.1 million/$5,278	$2 billion/$1.2 million
U.S. News ranking 2018	25th in National Universities	37th in Regional Universities Midwest	6th in National Liberal Arts Colleges
Acceptance rate (undergrad)	22%	89%	9%

Source: Unless otherwise noted, data is from *US News & World Report*, National University Rankings, accessed December 19, 2017, https://www.usnews.com/best-colleges/rankings/national-universities.

*Rankings by total research and development expenditures, National Science Foundation; accessed December 21, 2017, https://ncsesdata.nsf.gov/profiles/site?method=rankingBySource&ds=herd.

†Numbers from respective university websites.

lege on the West Coast.[37] Its name comes from its original location in the town of Pomona, California. Pomona is a member of the Claremont Colleges, a unique consortium similar to the structure of Oxford and Cambridge in the UK. Two graduate schools and five undergraduate colleges—the others are Scripps College, Claremont McKenna College, Harvey Mudd College, and Pitzer College—are situated on adjacent campuses, which promote joint use of facilities such as libraries and cross-registration among students. This gives Pomona students access to opportunities that would be difficult to maintain for a school with an enrollment below 2,000. The college prides itself on small classes and exceptionally close working relationships between faculty and students. About half of Pomona students participate in undergraduate research, and a similar percentage study abroad each year. Many win postgraduate scholarships. In conjunction with Pitzer College, Pomona fields twenty-one athletic teams, which participate in NCAA Division III. The teams are called the Sagehens. See table 2.5 for additional information on Pomona.

American colleges and universities vary considerably in their governance, size, wealth, tuition, selectivity, and focus on research versus focus on teaching, among other differences. In the next chapter, we will go inside and look at the structure of academic institutions, including colleges of arts and sciences and professional schools. We will also discuss degree programs, academic centers, and the nature of a curriculum and how it is changed.

3

Inside the Black Box
Schools, Centers, Degrees, and Curricula

Now that we have described the different kinds of colleges and universities, let's talk about what's inside them. What kinds of schools or colleges are found inside universities? What is a center or institute? What exactly is a degree? What is a curriculum, and how are curricula developed? What are some important administrative units? How is teaching and learning done today?

The College of Arts and Sciences

The College of Arts and Sciences, or the College of Liberal Arts—also known simply as the college—is usually the oldest and largest academic unit on campus. In baccalaureate schools like Pomona and the Air Force Academy, the college makes up the entire academic enterprise and often has a large number of departments. At the University of North Carolina at Chapel Hill and Pomona, the college has nearly fifty academic departments; the Air Force Academy (which does not use the designation of "college") has twenty-nine; the University of Wisconsin–Eau Claire has twenty-five. In some universities, arts and sciences comprise two or more units. For instance, Carnegie Mellon University has the College of Fine Arts, the Dietrich College of Humanities and Social Sciences, and the Mellon College of Science.

The intellectual scope of the typical college is vast, but the academic departments that fall under the college can be sorted into a few broad groups: natural sciences and math, social sciences, and arts and

Table 3.1. Typical Academic Departments in Colleges of Arts and Sciences

Natural Sciences and Mathematics	Social Sciences	Arts and Humanities
Biology	Anthropology	Art
Chemistry	Asian studies	Classics
Computer science	Economics	English
Environmental science	Geography	Foreign languages
Geology	Political science	History
Mathematics	Psychology	Music
Physics	Public policy	Philosophy
Statistics	Sociology	Women's studies

humanities. Table 3.1 shows some sample departments in each group.[1] Departments may be as small as half a dozen faculty or as large as eighty. College faculty meetings can include poets and physicists, classicists and chemists.

Because of both the size of the college and the centrality of many of its disciplines (such as mathematics and philosophy) to the history of academic thought, arts and sciences faculty often think of the college with good reason as the core of the university. Faculty are focused more on pure knowledge than on the use of knowledge that characterizes professional schools. In most universities, the majority of undergraduate students are in the college, so the college is at the center of many arguments about higher education, including the focus on job-related skills versus broader education, the alleged liberal bias of faculty, the use of graduate students (especially those from overseas) as instructors, and the influence of tenure on the behavior of professors.[2]

Professional Schools

Over time, universities have created professional schools to complement the college of arts and sciences. These schools (especially law and medicine) often focus on graduate students. But schools of business, engineering, and nursing often offer undergraduate degrees as well. Professional schools are closely aligned with their respective professions and compete for students, faculty, and prestige with professional schools at other universities. Faculty at these schools often worked in

Table 3.2. Examples of Professional Schools at Four Universities

Professional School	Carnegie Mellon	Gonzaga	Wisconsin–Eau Claire	UNC–Chapel Hill
Business	X	X	X	X
Computer science	X			
Dentistry				X
Education		X	X	X
Engineering	X			
Information/library science	X			X
Journalism				X
Law		X		X
Medicine				X
Nursing		X	X	X
Social work				X

the profession and may continue to be involved, for example, as consultants, or in the case of schools of medicine, dentistry, and nursing, as clinicians. Professional schools often use adjunct faculty from the profession to complement their tenure-track faculty (see chapter 5). These schools may or may not have departments, but even when they do the faculty identify more with the overall school than is generally the case in arts and sciences, where departmental affiliation is stronger. Table 3.2 provides examples of professional schools at the four universities described in chapter 2.[3]

Despite the differences between the college of arts and sciences and professional schools, there are some similarities in their areas of focus. For example, economists may be found in either the college or the business school or both; biochemistry may be in the college or in the medical school; both law school and political science faculty study the Constitution, and so on. The main difference is the commitment of professional school faculty to preparing students to flourish in a specific professional environment, as opposed to the broader focus of college faculty.

Centers and Institutes

Many universities have created centers or institutes (the terms are interchangeable) to promote research, education, and service in specific areas. Centers and institutes are often interdisciplinary (they span several academic departments) and funded through external grants. They are generally led by a faculty member as the center director, with a professional staff whose number depends on the size of the center. Centers can be as small as a few faculty members or as large as hundreds. Faculty may be primarily associated with a center, but more often their primary affiliation is with their home department(s).

American colleges and universities host an incredibly wide range of centers and institutes. Here are some examples:

- The Center for Global Engagement at Gonzaga University has as its vision to "advance Gonzaga University as a national leader in developing innovative programming that teaches the skills, attitudes, and knowledge necessary for our graduates to become reflective and ethical leaders in our increasingly interconnected world."[4]
- The Center for Communication Disorders at the University of Wisconsin–Eau Claire "offers speech, language and hearing services to the entire Chippewa Valley community."
- The Carolina Population Center at UNC–Chapel Hill is "a community of scholars and professionals collaborating on interdisciplinary research, methods, and training that advance understanding of population issues." Over 300 people — faculty, staff, and students — are affiliated with the center.
- The Center for the Neural Basis of Cognition at Carnegie Mellon University and the University of Pittsburgh "leverages the strengths of the University of Pittsburgh in basic and clinical neuroscience and those of Carnegie Mellon in cognitive and computational neuroscience to support a coordinated cross-university research and educational program of international stature." Several hundred people are associated with the center.
- The Air Force Academy Center for Character and Leadership Development "aims to facilitate programs and activities throughout all aspects of cadet life, which help cadets develop [their] internal moral compass. . . . The Center's activities and initiatives are firmly grounded in its conceptual framework for character and leadership development, creating an environment where cadets and faculty alike 'Own, Engage, and Practice' the

habits of honorable thoughts and actions in line with an identity of a leader of character."

Centers provide the structure needed for interdisciplinary work. Faculty who work in centers are situated similarly to businesspeople who work in matrix organizations, with the potential tension between center directors and department heads that this implies. Universities benefit from centers being, at least in theory, temporary. While some centers last for decades, others come and go, and it is much easier to close a center or institute than a school or college.

What Degrees Do Colleges and Universities Offer?

Colleges and universities (including community colleges and for-profit institutions) have the unique ability to confer academic degrees, which are a particular type of credential. The authority to award degrees is granted by the government, in most cases at the state level. This is because the Constitution does not grant to the federal government responsibility for education, with limited exceptions.[5]

The most common degree in colleges and universities is the bachelor's degree, which is often referred to simply as a "college degree." This degree has of course become the entry-level requirement for many if not most jobs in the contemporary economy. It comes in two variations, the bachelor of arts (BA) and the bachelor of science (BS). While these two are more similar than different, a BA degree generally represents more breadth of study and somewhat less depth in a particular field, while the BS degree has the opposite characteristics. In general, students who major in the humanities or social sciences are more likely to receive a BA, while those who major in science and technology are more likely to receive a BS.

The attainment of any degree is dependent on successful completion of a curriculum, which is the set of courses and extracurricular experiences specified by the faculty for that degree. The curriculum leading to a bachelor's degree is nominally four years, or eight semesters, which includes courses required for all students and courses specific to the major. Students pursuing a bachelor's degree usually start with a course of study lasting about two years, often called the general education (or gen ed) curriculum. This curriculum is a prerequisite for all majors and includes representative courses from a wide range of disciplines.[6] Gen ed courses are broken into different groups, and students are required to take courses in each group, so as to receive a broad liberal arts education.[7] In the final two years, students take more courses in their major area of study while often completing their general education requirements and perhaps also taking courses toward a minor. A minor involves a set of courses in a particular field of study that number roughly half those required for a major.

In quantitative terms, the requirements for a bachelor's degree often involve the successful completion of 120 credits of coursework (using the common model of three credits per course). A hypothetical student who proceeded in a steady manner through the curriculum would take five courses and complete 15 credits per semester and 30 credits per year for four years. Of course, in order to graduate the student would need to take the right credits. Perhaps half of these credits would be in the general education curriculum (and even these would have to be the *right* gen ed credits) and another 25 percent or so of the credits would be earned in the major, with the remainder devoted to a minor or simply to electives. Colleges and universities vary quite a bit in terms of how specific the requirements are for graduation, with most identifying broad areas and allowing students to choose within each area.

Moving up the academic ladder, the next degree is the master's degree. Master's degrees may be offered either by the College of Arts and Sciences or by one of the professional schools. Master's degrees from professional schools are sometimes referred to as professional degrees. Because courses for these degrees are offered almost entirely in a single department or professional school, they vary considerably, and the control over the curriculum is much more decentralized than is the case for the bachelor's degree. The most frequently earned master's degrees are in business (for example, master of business administration, or MBA), education (such as master of arts in teaching, or MAT), and the health professions (for example, master of public health, or MPH). These three types of degrees represent about 60 percent of all master's degrees conferred.[8] Higher education has witnessed tremendous growth over the past four decades in students earning professional degrees, with as many master's degree students today as there were earning their bachelor's degree in the 1960s.[9] A master's degree may be completed in as little as one year or as many as three or four years. Because many students who pursue master's degrees are already working, part-time and online master's programs are increasingly popular.

Most doctor of philosophy (PhD) students attain their master's degrees as part of their doctoral programs. We will discuss the PhD degree in chapter 5, in the context of how students become faculty members. Professional doctoral degrees include juris doctor (JD), doctor of medicine (MD), doctor of dental surgery (DDS), doctor of dental medicine (DMD), and doctor of pharmacy (PharmD).

How Is a Curriculum Developed? How Is It Changed?

Curricula at any level are developed, and can be changed, only by the faculty.[10] This is among the perquisites of the faculty that come under the framework of academic freedom (chapter 5) and faculty governance (chapter 6). Curricula in arts and sciences evolve as new areas of study and ways of thinking replace old ones. Many ongoing curricular changes are driven by an enhanced understanding of how students learn. Curricular changes in professional schools are often driven by changes in the profession. For example, business schools added courses in e-commerce and online marketing as these areas exploded. Of course, curriculum change has to be done with an eye toward accreditation standards (chapter 4).

How and how often curricula are changed depends on the type of degree. A small professional school could add or remove a required course by a faculty vote or an action of the curriculum committee from one year to the next. At the other extreme, the general education curriculum in the College of Arts and Sciences can literally take years and scores of meetings to change. This is not surprising, as such curricular change can affect thousands of students and hundreds of faculty and can lead to issues in the office of the registrar, in advising, and so on. Curriculum change also usually means that students in different cohorts (class years) are subject to different graduation requirements, which increases the complexity of the work of anyone advising students or keeping track of their progress.

It is worth mentioning the political component of curriculum development and change. At one level, faculty focus on what students need to learn to be successful people and citizens. At another level, they realize that if a course in their area is not required in the new curriculum, the number of faculty in their area may be held flat or even decline in the future. The key to the curriculum change process for faculty is therefore to use the motivation provided by the latter concern to inspire arguments couched in terms of the former. Faculty meetings on curriculum change where all of this takes place can be operatic in both tone and length.

What Are Some Key Administrative and Student Support Roles?

While faculty play the central role in the education of students, many staff members work closely and conscientiously with students and faculty to support the educational mission of the institution. These units have different names in different places, but the work they do is similar. In addition to the advice they receive from faculty, students benefit from working with academic advising to better understand the curriculum and the choices among courses, majors, and minors they can make. The career services unit helps students to think about their career aspirations and perhaps to connect with alumni in various fields. The office of counseling services provides mental health support to students and has been an area of growth on many campuses over the past few years. The registrar's office plays a key role in keeping track of credits and grades, student eligibility, course scheduling, transcripts, and a wide range of related issues. The student retention office analyzes data on student success and institutes programs intended to help students remain in college and graduate. Residence life is responsible for all elements of student housing, including building, programming, and behavioral issues. Student health often operates a clinic on campus and provides health information and health care to students.

How Have Teaching and Learning Changed since You Were in School?

While this book is not primarily about teaching and learning, classroom activities often evoke vivid memories in businesspeople of their own college experiences, as we mentioned in the introduction. And classroom teaching represents the core activity at most colleges and universities. It's helpful to summarize some of the ways in which undergraduate teaching and learning have changed in the past few years.

Traditional teaching still takes place in large lectures for introductory courses, complemented by smaller discussion classes that are sometimes referred to as recitations and often are led by graduate student teaching assistants.[11] In the sciences, labs take the place of discussion sections. Upper-level classes are often characterized by smaller class sizes and more faculty-student interaction. Changes in teaching and learning are due in large part to advances in information technology. In many classrooms the focus has shifted from delivery of information to higher levels of learning, including integration of ideas and application of those ideas to practice.[12] In an influential book, George Kuh referred to many of these practices collectively as "high-impact educational practices."[13] It's interesting to note, however, that some of these approaches incorporate elements of older models; after several thousand years, it is difficult to find anything in higher education that is entirely new.[14] While research on the impact of these practices on graduation rates is not entirely conclusive, they are endorsed and utilized by many institutions.[15]

FIRST-YEAR SEMINARS

Recognizing that students in the traditional classroom model may not have the opportunity for consistent interaction with a faculty member for several years, colleges and universities have introduced first-year seminars into the curriculum. The Gardner Institute defines a first-year seminar as "a small group [fewer than twenty-five] of first-year students ... engaged in study and research under a member of the faculty and meeting regularly to exchange information and hold discussions."[16] Seminars may be explicitly focused on the transition from high school to college or may be focused on a specific topic, which could be in virtually any academic area. They may be mandatory or voluntary. The Gardner Institute reports that the vast majority of four-year academic institutions now offer first-year seminars, and indeed they are available at Carnegie Mellon University, Gonzaga University, Pomona College, UNC–Chapel Hill, and the University of Wisconsin–Eau Claire. Evidence suggests that institutions offering first-year seminars have increased their retention rates for students.[17]

THE FLIPPED CLASSROOM AND OTHER STRUCTURAL INNOVATIONS

The idea behind the flipped classroom is that the activities traditionally done inside the classroom are done outside, and vice versa. More specifically, students may watch a recorded lecture online the evening before class and then engage in discussion or problem-solving in the actual class. This approach is sometimes justified using Bloom's taxonomy of learning, which organizes learning activities from lowest (remembering) to highest (creating).[18] The logic is to do the higher-level activities, such as assimilating knowledge, in class with the support of the professor and other students and to do the lower-level activities, such as reading the material for the first time, outside of class.[19]

In the past few years, faculty at a number of institutions, including UNC–Chapel Hill, have moved well beyond the flipped classroom model. The enhanced model is characterized by concepts such as active learning and increased course structure that have been shown to improve student learning outcomes.[20] High-structure courses may include, for example, frequent graded preparatory assignments and review assignments as well as significant in-class engagement of students (as much as 40 percent of course time or more). These structural changes may lead students to spend more time on their course and to spread out this time more effectively, to understand the class as a collaborative community, and to increase the perceived value of the course to students. In an interesting study of this approach, Sarah L. Eddy and Kelly A. Hogan were able to show growth in student achievement and moreover that achievement gains were different for different groups of students, with first-generation and African American students improving the most.[21]

Accommodating this new approach to teaching often involves changing the design of classrooms. At UNC–Chapel Hill, Greenlaw 101 has served as the model for classrooms to facilitate the new approach. As can be seen in figure 3.1, the instructor can walk among the students rather than remaining confined to the front of the room. The students are also seated in discussion pods with chairs that roll and swivel, so they can look in any direction and quickly switch from listening to the professor to discussing a problem in small groups. One of the most striking elements of the new classroom design is the number of screens, which not only can show several different videos or slides at the same time but also can be controlled by faculty or even students from their mobile devices.

3.1. Greenlaw 101, lecture hall for the twenty-first century, University of North Carolina College of Arts and Sciences, January 20, 2016. The photo features UNC chemistry professor Cheryl Moy, one of the early users of this classroom. Professor Kelly Hogan is to the right. (University of North Carolina at Chapel Hill)

SERVICE LEARNING

Service-learning courses engage students in community service projects in order to pursue educational objectives. This approach to education reflects integration of both goals and student activities. In terms of goals, service learning seeks both student development and community enhancement. At the activities level, service learning involves community engagement work, faculty instruction, and student reflection.[22] Service learning can be seen as a type of real-world case study, but instead of reading the cases, the students are living them in real time. This is faithful to an important goal of case studies—that student learning should be grounded in real-world issues and decisions. Students are often familiar with service learning, as it is increasingly used in high schools.

At the University of Wisconsin–Eau Claire, completing thirty hours of service learning is a requirement for graduation. The university states, "Service-Learning is an opportunity for students at UW–Eau Claire to give back to the local community, or their home community. It provides a way to learn skills, investigate careers, and build a personal network. Service-Learning makes education a collaborative effort; students benefit society by exercising the rights and responsibilities of citizenship."[23]

Many design options exist for service-learning courses. Students may engage with the community either as individuals or in teams. The projects may be as short as a few weeks or as long as a year or more. The projects may be identified by the instructor or by the students. Engagement may be part of one course, represent an entire course, or even span several courses. In each case, however, reconciling real-world issues with academic perspectives is at the heart of service learning.[24]

UNDERGRADUATE RESEARCH

Undergraduate research is defined as "an inquiry or investigation conducted by an undergraduate student that makes an original intellectual or creative contribution to the discipline."[25] This approach breaks the traditional mold in which research is the sole province of faculty and graduate students, with undergraduates playing at most bit parts. Undergraduate research can be in virtually any discipline and helps undergraduates play the lead roles in research: doing the literature review, designing the study, collecting the data, and interpreting the results.[26]

Often universities provide expos for students to share their research results. We have seen scores of such presentations, often summarized on posters, and have been consistently impressed by what undergrads can achieve given the opportunity. Research can help students become informed consumers of research and, while this is not the main goal, no doubt leads some students to pursue a PhD and a research career. Undergraduate research has become pervasive in American higher education: the Council on Undergraduate Research counts over 650 institutional members and nearly 10,000 individual members.[27]

A project conducted at Carnegie Mellon could be characterized as both service learning and undergraduate research. Students in the Dietrich College of Humanities and Social Sciences created and presented to the Pittsburgh City Council a report and planning tool for use of vacant land in the city. The tool is a decision tree that identifies areas of poverty and provides options for land use to enhance the areas, such as increasing access to job opportunities and health and wellness centers. The eight students worked as a team and were advised both by city council members and CMU faculty.[28]

ONLINE LEARNING

The online approach to teaching and learning can be seen as an outgrowth of correspondence courses, which universities have offered for many years to students who are unable to come to campus. One of our grandfathers took correspondence courses to become a coal mine electrician in the 1930s. In these courses, students would read books as directed by the college and mail in homework assignments to be graded and mailed back by the instructor. There was often no other interaction between students and professors and no interaction among students, who may have been scattered over hundreds or even thousands of miles. The huge advantage offered by correspondence courses was the ability to complete a course or even a degree without leaving home or, for older students, leaving one's job.

Online learning marries the basic framework of correspondence courses to the connectivity available via the Internet. Students still access readings, but they may also view recorded lectures or engage in interactive demonstrations. These learning methods, which can be done anytime the student wishes, are termed "asynchronous," reflecting another advantage shared with correspondence courses. But contemporary online learning also holds the promise of synchronous methods, which require students to participate in class activities at a specific time. While this is a disadvantage from a convenience standpoint, it opens the door to interaction with classmates not possible with earlier methods. Furthermore, synchronous learning may take place at any time of the day and is often offered in the evening or at night, when students have finished work and, in many cases, family responsibilities.

In some online programs, students can interact with one another and the instructor almost as if they were in the same classroom (see figure 3.2). This instructional format uses technology platforms that allow for video and audio feeds to be shared among class members in real time. Students in such programs have told us that they feel that they have met and worked directly with one another; when they meet in person, it has the sense of a reunion, not an introduction.

There are of course many variations in how colleges and universities have implemented online learning. They may develop, deliver, and market the courses themselves or may partner with a private firm to do so. They may offer degrees entirely online or as a hybrid with some in-person requirements. (Many faculty express concern about someone getting a degree from a university without ever setting foot on campus,

3.2. Synchronous learning in a virtual classroom. (MBA@UNC and
UNC Kenan-Flagler Business School)

but this is becoming increasingly common.) They may introduce online components into traditional classes, perhaps as part of a flipped-
classroom initiative.

As online programs emerged in the first two decades of the twenty-
first century, they were often controversial, as they were suspected of
being low quality, perhaps because the initial offerings in the online
category were from universities with limited reputations. But these
suspicions have largely gone away as more prestigious universities
have created such programs. More substantively, research has established that students can learn online as effectively as in conventional
courses—and in some cases even more effectively.[29]

MAKERSPACES

The last item in our summary of how education has changed in recent years is also the most recent; the first university-based makerspace
appeared at MIT in 2001. Makerspaces originated outside of universities as places with rapid prototyping equipment such as 3D printers
and laser cutters. The idea was to assist the expression of creativity
using equipment that individuals could scarcely afford. Over time
scores of universities have created such spaces on campus in order to
give students access to the tools needed to turn their ideas into reality.[30]
Makerspaces facilitate design education, as actually building models
has been shown to create better designs.[31] The informal environment
and social interaction of makerspaces also add to the educational ex-

3.3. IDeATe@Hunt, the makerspace at Carnegie Mellon University. (Carnegie Mellon University)

perience. Makerspaces on campus may be run by faculty, staff, or students. Interestingly, the library, despite its reputation for quiet, individual study, was the first location for many makerspaces on campus.

In conclusion, while one can still find places in universities with very traditional teaching and learning methods, the emergence of innovations such as first-year seminars, flipped classrooms, service learning, faculty mentored undergraduate research, online courses, and makerspaces has dramatically changed the nature of higher education.

How Are Colleges and Universities Influenced from Outside?
Regulation and Accreditation

We addressed in chapter 1 a major source of external control: rankings. At the college or university level, at the school level, and at the degree program level, academic leaders are compelled to take actions to enhance their rankings. Unlike the sources of influence we will discuss in this chapter, there is no statutory authority behind rankings, but their influence on academe is no less profound.

To the casual observer, it may appear that academic institutions control what happens on their campuses with little outside influence. But they are actually influenced by government agencies, court decisions, and accrediting organizations. In this chapter, we identify the most important external sources of influence.

Federal Influence on Higher Education

As Robert M. Hendrickson and his colleagues explain, "The federal government casts a long shadow over higher education."[1] Although the Constitution delegates primary responsibility for education to the states, the federal government plays a complex and important set of roles and has made a number of interventions in the higher education sector.[2] We will organize our discussion of federal influence around the three branches of government: executive, legislative, and judicial.

A number of departments in the executive branch influence American higher education. The U.S. Department of Education (ED), not surprisingly, plays several important roles, including administering grant and loan programs that support a great number of students. For example, the Pell Grant program provides grants to students from low-income families. Some of the department's loan programs include direct loans to students and PLUS loans to parents. The Perkins loan program has for decades provided low-interest loans to students with exceptional financial need, but this program was terminated in 2017.[3]

Readers may wonder why providing student aid is a means of influence over academic institutions. At one level, it simply means that institutions must meet the eligibility and reporting requirements of ED. But at a more profound level, it is this set of federal student aid programs that gives ED, and the federal government as a whole, its teeth, as the department has the ability to cut off aid to students at any institution. With few exceptions, this would put an institution's future in grave danger. For example, ED eliminated federal student aid for students at the Charlotte School of Law in 2017,[4] leading the school to close its doors. Fortunately for nonprofit institutions, this step is taken far more often for schools in the for-profit sector, mostly due to high student default rates on loans.[5]

ED also administers the Integrated Postsecondary Education Data System, better known by its acronym, IPEDS. This system mandates the collection, integration, and dissemination of vast amounts of information from all higher education organizations that receive federal funds.[6]

ED's Office for Civil Rights (OCR) enforces civil rights laws that prohibit discrimination and harassment on the basis of age, disability, race, color, and national origin. OCR also has responsibility for administering Title IX of the Education Amendments (1972), which regulates how universities address gender-based discrimination.[7] The initial impact of Title IX was to create equal opportunities for male and female student athletes. More recently, ED has interpreted Title IX to have significant implications for how universities address reports of sexual assault. Specifically, in a 2011 "Dear Colleague" letter, the department stated that it considers sexual assault to be a form of sex discrimination prohibited by Title IX. Institutions have gone to great lengths and expense — establishing new positions, offices, and procedures — to meet the requirements ED set out in the 2011 "Dear Colleague" letter. In November

2018 the Trump administration proposed new regulations, which were the subject of notice and comment:[8]

- A person accused of sexual misconduct would be guaranteed the right to cross-examine the accuser via an attorney or advocate.
- Colleges' responsibilities to investigate would be limited to cases in which there are formal complaints and the alleged incidents happened on campus or within an educational program or activity.
- Colleges would be required to act on a narrowed definition of sexual harassment.
- Colleges would have the option of using a higher standard of proof.
- Colleges would have more leeway to use mediation and other informal resolution procedures.[9]

The Trump administration contends that the previous Title IX provisions are expensive, inefficient, and unfair to the accused. It claims that the proposed new regulations provide "clarity for schools, support for survivors, and due process rights for all."[10]

Critics of Secretary Betsy DeVos's push to rescind the 2011 letter have requested that the Department of Education take time to consider the implications and possible harm to students.[11] They claim that the new regulations would fail survivors of sexual assault by

- reducing school liability by narrowing the definition of sexual assault and expanding religious exemptions (which also discriminate against LGBT students);
- allowing schools to choose the burden of proof required for sexual assault cases;
- dissuading survivors from reporting their assaults; and
- favoring the rights of the accused over the rights of survivors, for example, by requiring survivors to meet face to face with the attorney or advocate of the accused for cross-examination.[12]

Except in regard to standard of evidence, ED's proposed changes would not necessarily require colleges and universities to wholly revamp their Title IX policies and procedures.[13]

The Department of State regulates international student exchanges and also administers the Fulbright Program—which facilitates exchanges for professors and students—through its Bureau of Educational and Cultural Affairs. The Department of Veterans Affairs supports veterans attending college and determines the criteria by which institutions are eligible for students to attend using their GI Bill benefits.

Finally, the Department of Health and Human Services (through the National Institutes of Health), the National Science Foundation, and the Department of Defense (through the Defense Advanced Research Projects Agency) provide funding and shape the direction of biomedical, scientific, and defense-oriented research. We will explain how funded research works in chapter 7.

A 2015 study commissioned by Vanderbilt University and conducted by the Boston Consulting Group attempted to quantify the regulatory burden for colleges and universities as a result of the influence and oversight of executive branch departments. The study concluded that universities spend 3 to 11 percent of operating expenses on regulatory compliance and that faculty and staff devote between 4 and 15 percent of their time on activities associated with compliance.[14]

THE LEGISLATIVE BRANCH

The U.S. Congress was responsible for helping to create a large number of land-grant universities through the Morrill Acts of 1862 and 1090. The Morrill Act of 1890 extended benefits to former Confederate states and required states to establish land-grant universities for groups excluded by the admission policies of the institutions created under the original 1862 act. This led to the creation of many public historically black colleges and universities. Land-grant institutions include the University of Arizona, the University of Connecticut, and North Carolina State University, as well as historically black universities such as Florida A&M University, North Carolina A&T University, and Prairie View A&M University.[15]

Another high-water mark for congressional involvement in higher education was the Servicemen's Readjustment Act of 1944, more popularly known as the GI Bill, which provided funding for a large number of veterans returning from World War II to attend college. While in retrospect the bill seems obvious and uncontroversial, its passage was opposed by groups who wanted to limit benefits received by African American veterans, by groups who wanted benefits concentrated on those injured in the war, and by college presidents (including those of Harvard and the University of Chicago) who worried that a flood of academically unqualified veterans would cheapen their universities. In the end, however, President Franklin D. Roosevelt and his supporters in Congress prevailed. In its first decade, more than eight million veterans took advantage of the bill, which has been updated several times and continues to provide benefits to veterans today.[16]

The Higher Education Act of 1965 (which has now been reauthorized nine times) created the financial aid programs (Pell Grants, PLUS and Perkins loans) for generations of students and parents in need. The original act was part of President Lyndon Johnson's Great Society Agenda[17] and introduced a number of provisions to support colleges focused on underrepresented minority students, as well as programs to support international and foreign language study.[18]

The Jeanne Clery Disclosure of Campus Security Policy and Campus Crime Statistics Act (1990) requires colleges that receive federal funding to publish an Annual Campus Security Report. These reports must provide detailed information and statistics on several specific topics, including law enforcement authority, incidence of alcohol and drug use, and reported sexual assault and other crimes. The act also requires institutions to immediately alert their campus communities of any imminent dangers. It was championed by the family of Jeanne Clery,[19] an undergraduate student who tragically was murdered in her college dorm.[20]

Finally, Congress determines funding for all federal higher education programs under Title IV of the Higher Education Act and based on its role in creating and approving the annual federal budget.

THE JUDICIAL BRANCH

In this section, we focus on decisions by the Supreme Court that have had a significant influence on American higher education. These decisions relate to racial discrimination in admissions policies, affirmative action, student rights, and free speech.

DISCRIMINATION AND SEGREGATION IN COLLEGE ADMISSIONS

Two landmark decisions shaped admissions policies in American colleges and universities. *Plessy v. Ferguson* (1896) supported the "separate but equal" doctrine that allowed for black citizens to be excluded from white institutions and channeled into other lower-resourced institutions. Writing for the 8–1 majority, Justice Henry Billings Brown stated, "If one race be inferior to the other socially, the Constitution of the United States cannot put them on the same plane." While the case was unrelated to higher education (it was brought by Homer Plessy, a black man arrested for refusing to give up his seat to a white man on a train in Louisiana), the decision shaped admissions to academic institutions for the next six decades.

This doctrine was overturned in *Brown v. Board of Education* (1954), which ruled that separate schools were *not* effectively equal.[21] *Brown* was an amalgam of five cases in which several U.S. district courts had sided with school boards dictating segregation. Thurgood Marshall argued the case before the Supreme Court, claiming that separate school systems were inherently unequal and thus violated the Fourteenth Amendment's Equal Protection Clause. When the case was resolved in favor of the plaintiffs, Justice Earl Warren wrote for all the justices (the decision was unanimous), "We conclude that in the field of public education the doctrine of 'separate but equal' has no place. Separate educational facilities are inherently unequal."[22] Decades later, scholars continue to examine and debate the effectiveness of the *Brown* decision.[23]

AFFIRMATIVE ACTION

In the past few decades, racial issues in admissions have again become the subject of Supreme Court decisions. The fundamental question in all cases is whether colleges and universities can for any reason give consideration to race as part of a broad and holistic review of applicants. The Fourteenth Amendment's Equal Protection Clause is at the center of these cases, in which white (or more recently, Asian) plaintiffs claim that universities are violating their constitutional rights.

One of the earliest of these cases was *Regents of the University of California v. Bakke* (1978), in which Allan Bakke claimed that discrimination was the reason for his being declined admission to the medical school at the University of California, Davis. The Supreme Court found for Bakke in a 5–4 decision, stating that race could be a factor, but not the *only* factor, when making decisions on admissions. Quotas such as those used at Davis were thus deemed a violation of the Fourteenth Amendment.[24]

This general direction was reinforced in two 2003 cases involving the University of Michigan: *Gratz v. Bollinger* and *Grutter v. Bollinger*. In the former, the Court found for the plaintiff, criticizing the university's overly mechanized point system for handling diversity in undergraduate admissions. In the latter, Barbara Grutter argued that discrimination was responsible for her not being accepted into Michigan's law

4.1. *Source*: Tom Cheney/The New Yorker Collection/The Cartoon Bank.

school. This time, however, the Supreme Court upheld the admissions process (because race was one factor among many in a holistic, individualized review) and also emphasized that a diverse student body provides educational benefits.[25]

The Supreme Court cases known as *Fisher I* (2013) and *Fisher II* (2016) address the undergraduate admissions policies of the University of Texas at Austin. When the case was first filed, UT Austin admitted all applicants who graduated in the top 10 percent of their class at whatever Texas high school they attended. The remaining slots were awarded based on a point system that included race as a factor. Abigail Fisher was an applicant from Houston who was not accepted under either arrangement. She claimed that the use of race in the point system violated her Fourteenth Amendment rights. In *Fisher I*, the Supreme Court decided that UT's limited use of race in admissions decisions was not unconstitutional. However, the Court reinforced the principle used since *Bakke* that the use of race in college admissions must pass "strict scrutiny," meaning universities had to establish that they have a compelling interest in achieving a diverse student body and that there are no race-neutral alternatives that will successfully achieve the same levels of diversity without sacrificing academic quality.

The Supreme Court then sent the case back to the Fifth Circuit Court to be reviewed by this standard.[26] The Fifth Circuit Court again upheld the UT admissions process, and Abigail Fisher again appealed to the Supreme Court. In *Fisher II*, the Court determined that "since UT had sufficient evidence that its 'Top Ten' admissions policy based on class rank was not adequate to meet its diversity goals, it could permissibly consider a student's race as one factor in a broader assessment of qualifications."[27]

This area of law will continue to evolve with these and other cases.[28] Students for Fair Admissions recruits college applicants to join its membership list and promises to protect their confidentiality as it continues to explore and pursue further legal action on behalf of other plaintiffs.[29] For now, universities may use race as one factor in admissions decisions and within strict limits. They must continue to show that they seek the educational benefits of a diverse student body and that they are constantly evaluating race-neutral processes to produce this diversity.

STUDENT RIGHTS TO DUE PROCESS

In a series of decisions beginning with *Dixon v. Alabama State Board of Education* (1961), the courts established that public university college students' constitutional rights of free speech, due process, and protection from discrimination cannot be abridged by public institutions of higher education (which, essentially, are instrumentalities of the state governments that created them).[30] These decisions have important implications for student disciplinary procedures, in effect mandating academic institutions to follow due-process requirements. This requires, at a minimum, notice of the charges against the student and an opportunity for the student to be heard before any discipline is imposed. Prior to this decision, courts tended to defer to university authority with respect to students, so due process prior to taking disciplinary action was not required.[31]

FREE SPEECH

While many Court decisions on free speech do not involve academic institutions directly, they have significant implications for colleges and universities. The First Amendment to the Constitution protects free speech regardless of its content. As government institutions, public colleges and universities cannot abridge free speech, with very few exceptions, without violating the Constitution.[32]

Public institutions cannot make decisions on who can speak on campus based on their point of view or provide/withdraw support from student groups based on their invited speakers' point of view.[33] Nor can public colleges and universities regulate speech based on the response it may provoke; a "heckler's veto" could be used to discourage any type of unpopular speech. Public colleges and universities are actually required to provide adequate protection for speakers to ensure their First Amendment rights, which can be an expensive proposition for public institutions.[34] But in *Forsyth County, Georgia v. The Nationalist Movement* (1991), the Supreme Court ruled that government institutions cannot pass on these costs to the speakers or their supporters.

Public universities *can* regulate the "time, place, and manner" of speech as long as the restrictions are content neutral, are narrowly tailored to serve a government interest, and leave open other ample means of expression.[35] This precedent was established in *Linmark Associates v. Township of Willingboro* (1977), which involved the legality of the township's ban on For Sale signs on lawns. Academic leaders can also ensure that classes and other campus events go on without disruption and can take steps to discipline those who disrupt others' free speech rights in these settings.

One well-known exception to the First Amendment protection of free speech involves inflammatory speech intended to incite violence. In *Brandenburg v. Ohio* (1969), which involved the speech of a Ku Klux Klan leader, the Supreme Court established the "imminent lawless action" standard, saying that speech must "intentionally and effectively provoke a crowd to immediately carry out violent and unlawful action" to exempt it from free speech protection.[36]

The Court also ruled in *Chaplinksy v. New Hampshire* (1942) that so-called fighting words are not protected by the First Amendment. The case involved a member of the Jehovah's Witnesses who was arrested for calling someone a racketeer and a Fascist. This exception to free speech protections applies only to one-on-one speech of an intimidating nature that likely would lead to violence. It does not apply to someone speaking to a crowd in an auditorium. This exception is so narrow that the Supreme Court has not applied it in any other case.

Similarly, the Court has determined in *Watts v. United States* (1969) and *Virginia v. Black* (2003) that "true threats" of physical harm are not protected by the First Amendment, even if the speaker does not intend to carry out the threat. This exception does not apply to statements that cause emotional harm.

The First Amendment also does not create a right to harass others based on their race, sex, religion, sexual orientation, or any other characteristic. The proscription on harassment derives from Title VII of the Civil Rights Act (1964), as well as from Title IX of the Education Amendments, discussed earlier in this chapter. To make the difficult distinction between protected free speech and harassment, the latter is characterized by being unwelcome and discriminatory (based on a protected status such as race or gender) speech or conduct that is directed at an individual and is pervasive or severe enough that it undermines the targeted individual's access to educational programs.[37]

Campus speech codes have often been implemented to punish inappropriate speech, particularly "hate speech." In *Doe v. University of Michigan* (1989), the university's code was found to be unconstitutional. In fact, the courts have consistently ruled against the constitutionality of speech codes.[38] The Foundation for Individual Rights in Education publishes an annual report evaluating free speech on campuses and gives ratings to individual institutions. Interested readers can check the foundation's assessment of free speech on campuses.[39]

Erwin Chemerinsky and Howard Gillman, whose book *Free Speech on Campus* is a celebration of the First Amendment, explain, "History shows that campuses cannot censor or punish the expression of ideas or allow intimidation or disruption of those who are expressing ideas without undermining their core function of promoting inquiry, discovery, and the dissemination of new knowledge."[40] Clearly, the area of free speech at colleges and universities is deep and highly technical. An analysis of First Amendment rights is greatly dependent on the specific facts of each case. We urge board members and university leaders to listen to a wide array of campus opinions and consult regularly with their legal counsel for advice on specific issues in this domain.

State Influence on Higher Education

States influence the colleges and universities that operate within their borders in many ways. State influence primarily is felt by public colleges and universities, but it affects private institutions as well. While the specific nature of state influence over higher education varies among the states, there are enough similarities to allow for a general discussion.

As we noted in chapter 2, states with few exceptions provide the authority for colleges and universities—both public and private—to operate. States also have the authority to regulate *all* colleges and universities within their borders, as established by cases such as *New Jersey State Board of Education v. Board of Directors of Shelton College* (1982).[41]

But without question state influence is felt most strongly by public institutions.

Most states have created one or more higher education systems, intended to organize and manage the various public institutions of higher education and to optimize the higher education system as a whole.[42] (Many states also have a system for community colleges, which is out of scope for us and will not be counted in the descriptions below.) California has two systems, the California State University system and the University of California system. Texas actually has *six* systems, the largest of which are the Texas A&M system and the University of Texas system. Wisconsin, like many states, has only one system (which includes the University of Wisconsin–Eau Claire). The decision for states with many colleges is whether to deal with the complexity of having more than one system (such as California and especially Texas) or whether to deal with the complexity of having very different types of institutions within the same system (for example, Michigan, North Carolina, and Wisconsin).

The governance of public colleges and universities also varies from state to state. Some states (like Georgia and Wisconsin) have a single board responsible for all institutions, often called the board of regents. In New York the board of regents oversees not only the university system but public education at every level. The University of Michigan Board of Regents is responsible for the University of Michigan at Ann Arbor, Flint, and Dearborn but not for Michigan State University, which has its own board of trustees. A hybrid system is also used in North Carolina, where the board of governors is responsible for the entire system of universities, but each university has its own board of trustees.

Individuals come to these boards through a range of processes, primarily appointment by various parties (governors or state legislatures) or elections, differences that have implications for the loyalties and agendas of board members.[43] Many boards also have ex officio members, representing for example students or faculty. A 2010 survey of governing boards found that older white men with business backgrounds are the most frequent board members, that the average board size is eleven members, and that the average term length is six years.[44]

Whatever the specifics of institutional governance, state governments control a wide range of elements of public universities. States oversee an important part of the funding for public institutions, including operating funds and funding for capital expenses.[45] As we discussed in chapter 2, the amount of funding provided by most states is significantly less than it used to be, especially on a per-student basis. One of the effects of this defunding, which was exacerbated by the financial crisis of 2008, is a huge deferred campus maintenance backlog nationwide, which has been estimated at $30 billion.[46]

In general, however, reduced funding has not reduced the amount of influence wielded by states over their public universities, with the notable exception of the University of Virginia and other public universities in the state, which can retain enhanced autonomy as long as they meet a set of predetermined metrics.[47] In general, states regulate the amount of tuition that public institutions can charge and often attempt to keep tuition as low as possible, particularly for in-state undergraduate students. States often also control, directly or indirectly, the salaries of university employees. They additionally often maintain control over the ability of colleges and universities to pursue capital projects, decide whether a college can introduce a new degree program, and determine the percentage of out-of-state students that can be admitted.

Many states, in the name of accountability, require in-depth and regular reporting from their public universities. Report topics include academic performance metrics such as admissions, graduation rates, faculty teaching loads, and number of students per class and major. Financial and accounting metrics also are common. States increasingly use formulas based on metrics to determine university funding.[48]

A particular challenge to public colleges and universities, which is foreign to private institutions, is state regulations requiring open public meetings with prior notice (that is, sunshine laws). These laws generally were designed with state government in mind but apply equally to public universities. Exceptions are sometimes, but not always, made for the discussion of personnel or Family Educational Rights and Privacy Act–protected matters.[49] John V. Lombardi argues that open meetings encourage people at the university "to conduct their business off book, out of the formal processes, and off the public record [which] makes the visible process a less accurate reflection of the issues."[50] One area in which the desire of institutions for privacy and the state laws requiring public knowledge come into conflict is in the hiring of senior administrators, particularly college presidents. While public airing of their candidacies may deter candidates (especially presidents at other institutions) for these positions, universities in some states (such as Florida) have no choice but to make the process public.

Along similar lines, many states have freedom of information laws that require universities to release documents, notably copies of emails, to news organizations or ordinary citizens upon request. Beyond the potential embarrassment to individuals who write emails but forget that they may be made public, the collection, redacting (to remove personal or confidential information), and publication of documents for this purpose can be time-consuming and expensive.

Before we leave the topic of state control over academic institutions, it is worth pointing out that there is a structural conflict of interest between state legislators and governing board members on the one hand and academic leaders on the other. The former focus primarily if not exclusively on the universities' impact on the state, especially their efficiency in educating in-state undergraduates, while university leaders, whatever their level of dedication to their state (and in some cases it is quite strong), want to build a national or international reputation for their institution. This difference in focus and goals is at the heart of many conflicts between the two groups.

Accreditation of Colleges and Universities

Accreditation is the process by which colleges and universities are judged to meet or not meet current standards for higher education institutions.[51] The goal of accreditation is to provide an objective evaluation of the quality of institutions and to stimulate the raising of standards. While the entities that perform accreditation are private, they have tremendous influence over colleges and universities, because according to the Higher Education Act, federal financial aid can go only to students at accredited institutions. Who accredits the accreditors? The U.S. Department of Education. So, the accreditors' influence is actually derived from the federal government, and the accreditation process is voluntary in name only.

Accreditation operates at two levels: the institutional level and the specialized or programmatic level. At the institutional level, the government, accrediting organizations, and academic institution are linked together in a process with very high stakes. Institutional accreditation has evolved to focus on six regional accreditors recognized by the Department of Education: the Higher Learning Commission, the Middle States Commission on Higher Education, the New England Association of Schools and Colleges, the Northwest Commission on Colleges and

Universities, the Southern Association of Colleges and Schools, and the Western Association of Schools and Colleges.[52]

Specialized or programmatic accreditation applies to units within institutions, which could be as large as a school within a college or university or as small as an individual curriculum within a department. Professional schools are accredited by organizations such as the Association to Advance Collegiate Schools of Business, the American Bar Association, and the Liaison Committee on Medical Education, sponsored by the American Medical Association and the Association of American Medical Colleges. Individual departments within arts and sciences are also often accredited by specialized organizations such as the American Chemical Society and the Commission on Accreditation of the American Psychological Association. ABET (which formerly stood for Accreditation Board for Engineering and Technology but now is just the organization's name) is a programmatic accreditor for science, computing, and engineering.

The accreditation process plays out similarly at both the institutional and programmatic levels. The accrediting organization establishes and regularly updates criteria for institutions to meet in order to be accredited.[53] The institution prepares a self-assessment against the criteria established by the accrediting organization. Self-studies can easily run to hundreds and even thousands of pages. They are evaluated by a group of academic peers from other institutions, assembled by the accrediting organization. This group or a similar group then visits the campus for an on-site evaluation, generally for about two or three days. After the visit, the group makes a recommendation to the accrediting organization, which eventually is formally ratified by the accrediting organization and made public. At the institutional level, this process takes place every ten years. At the specialized level, the time period varies.

We have included accreditation in this chapter on external sources of influence, but accreditation leaders (who are professional employees) and evaluators (who are volunteers) all are drawn from the types of colleges and departments that are evaluated in the accreditation process. While accreditation is legitimized by the federal government, accreditation standards are established and maintained by members of the organizations being accredited. This appears to run the risk of "regulatory capture," which occurs when a government agency serves the interests of the industry it is supposed to regulate rather than the general public, generally through weakening of or inconsistent enforcement of regulations.[54] But accreditation at the institutional level is an expensive, time-consuming, and complex process, with incredibly detailed, even Byzantine, standards. It is hard to imagine, despite the makeup of the accreditors, that accreditation has been "captured."

At the school or program level, however, the dynamics are very interesting. Many of the standards put forward at this level—designed by members of the professional or disciplinary community—require considerable resources to be directed toward the programs being assessed. Lombardi concludes, "Associations focused on particular faculty guilds [academic disciplines] use accreditation to distort university funding priorities by demanding more equipment and space, more extensive support services, and lower student-to-faculty ratios than may actually be necessary for a quality product."[55] We were once told in serious tones by members of a faculty advisory group that they were concerned about the potential for declining ranking of a particular set of programs on campus. What did we need to do to manage this threat? Give them a bigger budget.

Additional Influences

While we have addressed the most important sources of external influence on colleges and universities, there are other outside groups that also shape the structure and behavior of colleges and universities. National organizations include the National Collegiate Athletic Association, the American Association of University Professors, and a number of labor unions that represent faculty and staff. The Foundation for Individual Rights in Education, identified earlier in this chapter, also falls into this category. Colleges and universities are also influenced by both local and national media, including newer forms of media (such as blogs) and social media (especially Twitter). Many universities wisely monitor their coverage in all of these media.[56] In his recollection of his time as president of Texas A&M University, Robert M. Gates (also former secretary of defense) identified alumni and sports fans as influential external constituencies.[57]

Finally, while our focus has been on how influence flows from outside the campus into academic institutions, influence certainly flows the other way as well. Colleges and universities—individually and collectively—undertake a number of activities to sway public policy. Collectively, they operate through organizations such as the American Council on Education, the Association of American Universities, and the Association of Public and Land-Grant Universities, all of which lobby for university interests in Washington. Larger colleges and universities also retain their own lobbyists, both in Washington and in their state capitals, to influence state and federal policy. Most universities also have added strategic communications or public affairs groups to affect communications and public perception of their institutions. And a sufficient number of institutions have utilized the services of public relations consulting firms, some of which have created a specialized practice area in higher education.

5
Who Are
the Faculty?

The faculty are, along with the students, at the center of university life. Faculty engage in educating students, advancing research, and providing service to university, community, and profession. The importance of these roles varies across institutional types and faculty appointments.[1] In this chapter, we will describe how people get to be faculty members, the variety of faculty ranks, and how faculty are evaluated and promoted. We will also talk briefly about the concepts of tenure and academic freedom. Finally, we will discuss what motivates faculty in their profession.

How Does Someone Become a Faculty Member?

People usually become faculty members by completing a doctor of philosophy (PhD) program. As discussed in chapter 2, only a small number of universities offer PhD programs, so by definition new faculty come from one of about 300 universities in the United States. However, a much smaller number of institutions (the exact number depends on the field of study) produce most of the PhD graduates who go on to be faculty.[2] Faculty also come from universities abroad, but more PhD students from around the world come to the United States for their doctorates; one study put the number at about 135,000 students at any one time.[3] Doctoral programs are significantly different from undergraduate and master's programs. They are more similar to apprenticeship programs, in which students learn the craft of academics and especially of research.[4] Graduate students typically gain experience in research (and sometimes teaching) under the tutelage of faculty members and also engage in small seminars and study groups. One major difference from other graduate programs is that most PhD students do not pay tuition. They generally receive stipends and tuition waivers that support their studies so they do not have to work outside of their program or take out loans. In return for this remuneration, graduate students teach, serve as teaching assistants (TAs), or work on research in their department. Stipends vary quite a bit across disciplines and are generally lowest in the humanities and highest in the sciences. Stipends in the range of $20,000 to $30,000 per year are common. The absence of tuition and the presence of stipends mean that doctoral programs are not profitable for universities, to say the least. However, PhD students play an important role in research (see chapter 7) and teaching (working well below market rate) and help to build the reputation of the university and its faculty.

PhD students generally spend from four to six years in a doctoral program. The first year or two are devoted primarily to coursework, in which students master the existing body of knowledge with an eye toward conducting research that will advance their discipline. For many students (certainly including us), this is a heady and somewhat overwhelming time and in this way somewhat like the first year of professional degree programs such as the juris doctor or master of business administration.

DOCTORAL COURSEWORK

PhD courses are generally small seminars with perhaps five or ten students and involve massive amounts of reading. Students who cannot handle this volume of reading quickly realize that they are probably not cut out for the academic life (this thought has doubtless occurred to all PhD students at some point). Class sessions are much more interactive and conversational than most undergraduate courses; faculty members engage students in deep discussions of the implications of the readings, considering how they add to what is known about a particular topic, what their methodological strengths and weaknesses are, and so on. Doctoral students soon discover that being quiet and passive in a seminar not only is nearly impossible but also can be career-threatening.

Beyond the obvious educational aspects of doctoral seminars, a number of other things are happening. First, students are getting socialized into the norms and culture of academics in general, their field in particular, and, even more specifically, the view of their field among the professors in their department. This deep dive into their discipline would include, for example, an examination of the benefits of one approach to research versus another. Second, each student's "stock" is rising or falling with his or her performance in each seminar. Faculty members quietly keep track of student performance and potential, which informs the next activity, the informal matching process that goes on between faculty and students within the program. This selection of sorts culminates in an agreement that a certain faculty member will be the doctoral adviser for a certain student, while other faculty members will serve on his or her dissertation committee.[5]

TRANSITION TO RESEARCH

As students enter the second and third years of their doctoral programs, they take fewer courses and spend most of their time conducting research with their professors. Research may grow out of an idea from the professor or from a student's own idea as expressed in a paper written for a course or through other engagement with the field. It is not uncommon for students to work with several faculty members at this stage, both to round out their education and to further the faculty adviser matching process (unless they have been admitted to work with a specific faculty member). If students are in a discipline where there is external funding, faculty members may begin to fund the students who work with them. Faculty with strong reputations, available funding, and interesting research projects are in a position to recruit the best doctoral students to work with them.

At several points in the PhD process, departments conduct reviews of their doctoral students. Students who do not appear to have high potential may be counseled out of the program. While the first few years of doctoral education are resource-intensive, requiring many hours of faculty mentoring, the final two or so years are much more so. Most PhD programs are small and highly competitive. Departments have strong incentives not to devote any resources to marginally performing PhD students, particularly as the students transition to research. One clear sign of limited promise for students is whether few if any professors are willing to work with them. Even then, however, faculty are sometimes reluctant to let students go, based on the personal relationships they have developed or perhaps on the hope that their performance might improve.

THE DISSERTATION

As students enter the fourth and fifth years of their programs, their attention turns almost exclusively to their dissertation, also known as the doctoral thesis. While what constitutes a dissertation differs significantly among fields, it is consistently seen as a major work of original research. Dissertations may be as short as a few dozen pages (such as in mathematics) or as long as several hundred pages (in the humanities or social sciences). In most fields in natural and social sciences, the dissertation involves collecting data in order to test a set of hypotheses, which are found to be either supported or not supported by the data. In the humanities, students write their dissertations with the goal that they will be published as books.

A faculty adviser and a committee made up of a handful of professors guide students in completing their dissertations. Two common milestones in the dissertation process are the proposal defense and the thesis defense. In the former, students seek the approval of their committee to undertake a specific research project for their dissertation. In the latter, students seek approval for the completed project. Both generally involve oral presentations before the committee and often other faculty and students. In general, once the dissertation committee signs off on the thesis defense, the student has effectively completed his or her PhD. Often this accomplishment is celebrated with fellow students and faculty members, who will delight in calling the student "Doctor." The eventual graduation ceremony—which students may or may not attend—is clearly secondary in importance to the dissertation defense.

Two other things are going on during this same period. The first— which may begin as early as the second year of the PhD program— is that students are expected to begin teaching, almost always at the undergraduate level, and often in introductory courses. While this practice is beginning to change, most doctoral programs place much more emphasis on students learning to do research than on learning how to teach. If a student is fortunate, he or she will receive some mentoring from faculty members or more senior students, or the university may have resources and programs to help PhD students learn how to teach.[6] If not, learning how to teach will be based more on past experience, observation, and trial and error, often to the dismay of the undergraduates in these doctoral students' courses. The focus of PhD programs on research over teaching is probably the biggest disconnect from what members of the general public expect, since they typically view professors primarily as teachers and not necessarily as researchers.

The second thing going on during the dissertation process is that PhD students begin looking for jobs. In some disciplines, the most common path is a postdoctoral fellowship (referred to commonly as a postdoc) for one or two years; in others, students go straight from their PhD programs to their first faculty job. This is another type of matching process, in which students generally will seek a tenure-track job at the most prestigious university possible, while universities try to find the strongest new PhDs who are interested in working for them.

THE JOB SEARCH

During the PhD job search,[7] a rough match usually occurs between the prestige of the doctoral-granting institution and the hiring institution, although of course some students move up or down in the pecking order based on the strengths or weaknesses that they possess going into the job search. The stronger the student, the more prominent the student's institution, adviser, and dissertation committee, the better the dissertation per se (as well as the ability of the student to publish and present his or her research), the better the student is likely to perform on the faculty job market. Other factors influencing job search success include the number of positions open at the time the student is looking, which is in turn a function of demand for the student's academic discipline as well as overall economic conditions.

Much has been written about the academic job market in the past few years.[8] For new PhDs, achieving a tenure-track appointment at a prestigious university has become very difficult, especially in the arts and humanities, in some of the social sciences, and even to some degree in the natural sciences. Students may take one or more postdoc positions, stay at their doctoral university longer, or accept a fixed-term adjunct or teaching position. Seeing these dynamics at close hand has led professors in a number of fields to actively discourage undergraduate students from pursuing a PhD.[9]

Newly minted PhDs also are increasingly taking jobs outside of academics for a variety of reasons, including better pay or simply the lack of opportunities in their particular field.[10] But since our focus here is on how people become faculty members at colleges and universities, we will not discuss these alternative PhD career paths.[11] We will note that the process of earning one's graduate degree can be stressful, and in some specific cases unhealthy. Numerous studies show that mental health disorders disproportionately affect graduate students. In a recent Harvard study,[12] 18 percent of PhD students experienced moderate to severe symptoms of anxiety and depression, more than three times the national average, and their mental difficulties actually were exacerbated by their participation in a graduate program. Further, their mental health symptoms worsened the longer they were enrolled in a doctoral program.

What Kinds of Faculty Members Are There?

We will describe three types of faculty members: tenure-track (or tenure-stream) faculty members, fixed-term faculty, and adjunct faculty.[13]

TENURE-TRACK FACULTY

Tenure-track faculty appointments traditionally have been the default in universities, but tenure-track positions are becoming increasingly rare, for reasons we will explain. There generally are three ranks through which tenure-track faculty progress: assistant professor, associate professor, and full professor (or simply professor).[14] New tenure-track faculty most often are hired as assistant professors.[15] These junior faculty have several years (six is common, but as many as nine is not unheard of) to amass a record that will merit being promoted to associate professor and awarded tenure. Faculty usually receive some sort of review each year, with at least one significant interim review at about three years. It is no exaggeration to say that for assistant professors, putting themselves in position to merit promotion and tenure is their primary preoccupation during this time. Remember that they have already spent about six years in a PhD program, perhaps one or more years in a postdoc, and now about six years as an assistant professor. This means that they may be in their mid-thirties or older by the time the career-defining tenure decision is made.

Promotion and tenure decisions are considered to be among the most important decisions made by universities and are taken very seriously. While practices vary quite a bit from one college or university to another, a typical process would be as follows: Candidates put together a package that summarizes their accomplishments in research, teaching, and service (to the department, the university, the profession, and/or the public). Since not much service is expected from assistant professors—and in fact they are usually actively discouraged by their mentors from spending much time on it—we will focus on the research and teaching elements of a faculty candidate's tenure package.

At research-intensive universities, the candidate's research performance will be the primary determinant of tenure.[16] The tenure package will include a statement from the candidate about his or her research, copies of the candidate's research papers, and summaries of his or her levels of funding in fields in which this is relevant. The package also will include a set of letters from well-known professors at peer universities who have been asked to assess the candidate's research (see chapter 7 for a description of peer review), and to make a recommendation as to whether the candidate should receive promotion and tenure. The question framed to these individuals is sometimes, "Would this candidate be likely to receive promotion and tenure at your institution?" It is difficult to imagine a business in which executives at competing organizations would be asked to weigh in on a promotion decision, but this is standard practice in colleges and universities. Moreover, the professors asked to write these letters spend significant amounts of time reading and considering the research of the candidate. As we discussed in chapter 1, this practice demonstrates the extent to which faculty see themselves as members of an academic community that is much larger than their own university, and to which they owe significant allegiance.

Promotion and tenure packages also include lists of courses candidates have taught and evidence of success in teaching, which may be at the undergraduate, master's, or doctoral level. At institutions whose primary mission is teaching (such as baccalaureate colleges), indicators of teaching success primarily will drive promotion and tenure decisions. Course evaluations by students are among the most common indicators of faculty teaching performance, even though their validity has been seriously questioned in a number of studies.[17] Course evaluations are seductive due to their apparent objectivity and their inherently quantitative nature, which allows for comparisons among faculty members. But the tendency of students to be influenced by such factors as the gender of the professor or the easiness of grading has made institutions more cautious in relying on course evaluations too heavily.

In many universities, faculty teaching performance further will be assessed by classroom visitations from other faculty, who write memos summarizing their impressions. If the faculty member being evaluated has created teaching materials, especially innovative materials, such as simulations or case studies, these also will be included in his or her tenure package, as will the list of doctoral students supervised by that faculty member (if the university has a doctoral program) and the universities that have hired these students.[18]

Once the promotion and tenure package is created, it is reviewed in a fixed order by a series of committees and individuals, the specifics of which vary from one institution to another and from one academic department to another. A typical set of reviewers would include a department committee, the department chair, a school or college committee, the dean of the school or college, a university-level committee, the provost or the president (or both), and perhaps the governing board (which rarely does more than ratify what has already been decided by the aforementioned groups). At each level, the individual or group writes a memo summarizing conclusions about the candidate and containing a recommendation on whether he or she should be promoted with tenure. If the department chair or dean does not recommend promotion, the process may end there. If the promotion process nevertheless moves forward, the likelihood of success is certainly much lower.

What frequently is not appreciated outside of higher education is the high stakes associated with this decision.[19] If the outcome is positive, the candidate will be promoted to associate professor and can continue uninterrupted with his or her academic career but with the critically important attainment of tenure and all the benefits that this status confers. If the tenure decision is negative, however, the candidate's appointment at the institution will expire, generally about a year after the decision, and he or she will have to leave the university. In this way, tenure decisions are similar to "up or out" decisions made in a number of professional service firms. During their final year, unsuccessful promotion and tenure candidates generally will seek jobs in other universities, usually at less prestigious schools. Sometimes a research university will retain faculty members as fixed-term professors, often due to their teaching ability.

WHAT IS TENURE?

Tenure is a simple concept. Being tenured means that, barring unusual circumstances (including a failure to perform one's duties at a

"Today, class, I'm proud to announce my tenure."

5.1. *Source:* Farley Katz/The New Yorker Collection/The Cartoon Bank.

minimally acceptable performance level), a professor will be able to remain employed by the university indefinitely (and in fact, tenure is technically considered "indefinite tenure"). Since universities are legally proscribed from setting retirement ages for faculty, this arrangement could be in place for three or even four decades.

However, out of concern for the possibility of faculty members using their tenured status to reduce their performance, many universities have instituted some form of post-tenure review, in which a faculty member seen as not meeting the minimum criteria for performance can be dismissed. This type of dismissal happens rarely, but it does occur. The other circumstances in which tenured faculty can be dismissed include very serious financial problems at the institution, the closing of an academic program, or behavior by a faculty member that violates expectations of ethical or professional behavior. All of these circumstances are relatively rare.

The practice of awarding tenure grew from a desire among universities to protect their faculty from interference in their research, especially any interference that is ideologically motivated.[20] This principle is generally known as academic freedom, and its importance in the academy cannot be overstated. The American Association of University Professors (AAUP) is seen as the guarantor of academic freedom in the United States. In 1940, the AAUP, in conjunction with the Association of American Colleges and Universities, created the Statement of Principles on Academic Freedom and Tenure.[21] This version replaced earlier formulations in 1915[22] and 1925 and was given additional interpretation by the AAUP in 1970. The essential agreement underlying this document has been sustained for many decades and repeatedly endorsed by colleges, universities, and professional organizations. Keith Whittington in the *Chronicle of Higher Education* explains, "The paramount obligation of university trustees [as outlined in the statement] is 'to refrain from attempting to impose their personal opinions upon the teaching of the university' and to respect that they have 'no moral right to bind the reason or the conscience of any professor.'"[23] The core of the argument for academic freedom can be found in the 1940 statement: "Institutions of higher education are conducted for the common good [which] depends upon the free search for truth and its free exposition. Academic freedom is essential to these purposes and applies to both teaching and research. Freedom in research is fundamental to the advancement of truth."[24] So the argument for tenure essentially is that university professors best serve the public good through the ability to pursue truth freely (without political or administrative interference), and tenure is how this public service is guaranteed.

It is worth noting that the AAUP statement also identifies responsibilities for professors, which go along with the privileges of academic freedom and tenure: "College and university teachers are citizens, members of a learned profession, and officers of an educational institution. When they speak or write as citizens ... their special position in the community imposes special obligations. As scholars and educational officers, they should remember that the public may judge their profession and their institutions by their utterances. Hence they should at all times be accurate, should exercise appropriate restraint, should show respect for the opinion of others, and should make every effort to indicate that they are not speaking for the institution."[25] Some who criticize the idea of tenure are troubled by the fact that not all faculty live up to these responsibilities.

ASSOCIATE, FULL, AND DISTINGUISHED PROFESSORS

Associate professors are in the middle rank of the tenure track. Most have achieved tenure and will spend several years (at least) as associate professors before being considered for promotion to full professor. They are now generally part of the process that determines whether other faculty will receive promotion and tenure. They can cease worrying whether they will have to leave their university and find a new position in the near future. Beyond this status, however, not much has changed. Associate professors likely will earn more than assistant professors, but the size of this salary gap varies and may be quite small, especially where salary compression exists due to increases in starting salaries for assistant professors. Thus it is common for associate professors to have an "Is this all there is?" moment after achieving promotion and tenure. After a celebration and a deep breath, most simply go right back to work.[26] This is another area where the general public's understanding of academic life can be misinformed.

After a few years, associate professors are usually considered for promotion to full professor. This promotion relies on sustained performance in research and teaching, with perhaps some additional consideration of their service contributions. Service may include a departmental position such as director of undergraduate education, engagement in faculty governance, or membership on a university committee. The decision process for promotion to full professor is very similar to the one for promotion and tenure, with one enormous difference: the decision is not "up or out." If someone is turned down for promotion to full professor, they may simply remain at their institution as an associate professor with tenure. Moreover, they can go through the process again and may be successful the second (or, in rare instances, the third) time around.

Sometimes associate professors do not perform at a level to merit promotion to full professor. Usually this is because they do not continue to do research at the same level as before they were tenured. This drop in research productivity may be because they no longer are interested in research or can no longer successfully compete for funding or publication in academic journals. Sometimes faculty decide to put all of their energy into teaching, which will not lead to promotion to full professor in research-intensive universities. In any case, a relatively small number of associate professors stay at that rank for the balance of their careers; they are sometimes known as "terminal associate professors."

Full professors, as the term implies, are the senior members of their academic department. They generally are paid more than associate professors (with the same caveats as above) and are expected to set the academic direction for their department. They play key roles in attracting and mentoring new faculty and PhD students. They are the source of department chairs as well as deans and other senior members of university administration. When academics at other schools think about a department, the full professors are generally whom they think of as representing the department.

Finally, a small proportion of full professors become distinguished professors. This is an honor for which one generally must be nominated or identified by a department chair or dean as a meritorious candidate. Often distinguished professorships have been established by a gift from a donor for whom the distinguished professorship is named—for example, the Sarah Graham Kenan Distinguished Professor of Medicine.[27] The distinguished professorship usually comes with some financial resources, which may be added to the faculty member's salary or may provide research funding. Even within the category of distinguished professors, there are gradations. For example, university-level distinguished professors are more prestigious and often better funded than department- or school-level professorships. If you are a professor with a university-level distinguished professorship, you definitely have arrived.[28]

FIXED-TERM AND ADJUNCT FACULTY

So far we have focused on the various faculty ranks within the tenure track. But many faculty, and an increasing percentage over the past few years, are not on the tenure track. Some of these individuals are full-time faculty, who often are referred to as fixed-term (as opposed to indefinitely tenured) faculty. These faculty have contract lengths of one to three years, sometimes longer. While they may work at the same institution for many years, they never enjoy the job security, independence, or prestige of tenured professors. In research-intensive universities, fixed-term faculty often are those individuals who teach but do limited or no research. Some universities, such as UNC–Chapel Hill, recognize the critical role of fixed-term teaching faculty and assign levels of titles similar to those of tenure-track research faculty: teaching assistant professor, teaching associate professor, and teaching professor.[29] Fixed-term faculty also are more often than not assigned to student-support-related activities within their department, such as major advising or director of undergraduate studies. However, it is increasingly the case that research-active faculty may also be hired as fixed-term. Due to their full-time status, fixed-term faculty are employees of the institution and generally receive health insurance and other benefits.

The most contingent faculty are known as adjuncts. These faculty are not full-time and are hired to teach one or more courses in a given semester. While this title originally was used for people who had another job and lectured part-time for additional money or simply because they enjoyed it, adjuncts increasingly are faculty who would prefer to have a full-time or tenure-track position, but the position has not been offered to them. They receive relatively low pay (generally less than $5,000 per course, and often far less) and often do not receive any benefits. Sometimes they do not know until the last minute whether they will be called upon to teach a course in any given term, and they may be offered the opportunity to teach only when another faculty member has fallen ill or left the university suddenly. In parts of the country where it is possible, individuals may cobble together a nearly full-time job by teaching courses at two or more universities. Considering such scenarios,[30] it is easy to see why PhD students aspire to tenure-track positions.

While tenure-track faculty made up the majority of faculty in American universities in the last century, that percentage today has fallen below 40 percent.[31] Universities increasingly have used fixed-term and adjunct faculty to manage economic uncertainty, although this tendency varies widely by type of institution. Even in a low-paying department, granting tenure to someone in his or her thirties is a commitment of up to several million dollars. With growing uncertainty about virtually every source of revenue, universities have hedged their bets by hiring more contingent faculty members. Of course, there likely are noneconomic, and unforeseen, consequences of these hiring practices. It is difficult for contingent faculty to feel the same level of institutional commitment as tenured faculty members, and they may not have the time (or even the office space) to do any serious student advising.[32]

One important difference among types of universities and professors that we have not yet addressed is how much they teach. Most colleges and universities refer to this as "teaching loads." Tenure-track faculty in research-intensive universities may teach at most two courses per semester (three to four courses per academic year) or fewer if they have "bought out" some of their time with research grants.[33] Tenure-track faculty in non-research-intensive universities or fixed-term faculty in research universities may teach three or four courses per semester (six to eight courses per academic year). These differences in teaching loads indicate that the jobs of professors vary widely in terms of their focus on teaching and research.

How Are Faculty Paid?

Faculty in many disciplines are paid what is considered a nine-month salary, corresponding to the length of the conventional academic year.[34] Faculty generally have their total salary paid out over all twelve months of the year, so this nine-month arrangement is not obvious. This does not mean that faculty do not work in the summer, as expectations for ongoing research and course preparation would make this very difficult to pull off. It does mean that faculty can augment their compensation by generating research grants that pay their summer salary or by teaching in the summer.

Faculty compensation is a function of many factors. Academic discipline plays a large role, with faculty in professional schools and the sciences generally paid more on average than faculty in the arts and humanities. The nature of the institution itself also matters, as private schools often pay more than public schools, and within those categories more prestigious institutions generally pay more. Tenure-track faculty are paid more than fixed-term and adjunct faculty, and pay increases as one moves up the ranks from assistant to associate to full professor. Finally, a faculty member's performance influences his or her salary.

One element of compensation that may be surprising to business-people is the start-up package. From the outside this looks like a signing bonus, but this is misleading. It is funding made available to faculty joining a research university to set up their research labs, hire a team of graduate students, and the like in anticipation of their receiving external funding for their research later (see chapter 7). Start-up packages can run into the hundreds of thousands and even millions of dollars; this practice hinders universities with limited budgets from competing for the best faculty, especially in science, as they cannot afford to support these packages.

What Motivates Faculty Members?

It should be clear by now that faculty in American colleges and universities are a diverse group of individuals. They are in academic disciplines as diverse as physics and poetry. Some are in tenure-track positions; some are in adjunct positions. Some are nearing retirement; some are in their twenties. Some teach several courses per semester; others hardly teach at all. Can anything definitive be said about what motivates them?

Many of the job factors that motivate faculty are the same as those that motivate people in business or anywhere else. They want to be paid appropriately for their contributions and compensated fairly with respect to their colleagues at their own and other institutions. Sometimes faculty change universities to achieve higher pay, just as in any other job sector. They have families and mortgages. Some businesspeople believe that because academia is a type of calling (and presumably faculty could make more money in some other line of work), money is not important to faculty. This is simply not true, as anyone who has negotiated with faculty over salaries can easily attest. As with any other profession, salary is important, especially when you consider that "roughly 13 percent of Ph.D. recipients graduate with more than $70,000 in education-related debt, though in the humanities the percentage is about twice that. And for those who do secure an academic post, census data suggest that close to a third of part-time university faculty—many of whom are graduate students—live near or below the poverty line."[35]

Job advancement is important to faculty, especially those on the tenure track. Junior faculty (assistant professors) will work extraordinary hours—late nights, weekends, holidays—to enhance their chances of promotion and tenure. But this work ethic sometimes is difficult to distinguish from the passion that faculty have for their particular area of interest, whether it be teaching or research in their specific discipline. Faculty usually are happiest when they are engaged with colleagues and students in the work that they love. We have already noted that most faculty have spent upward of fifteen somewhat uncertain years to obtain a permanent position at an institution. Commitment to their discipline and passion to engage with students and colleagues are primary professional motivators. Further, faculty are motivated to share in discovery and the dissemination of knowledge. An esteemed economist and provost emeritus explains, "Our collective interest and primary motivation for pursuing and disseminating knowledge explains a characteristic of universities that some businesspeople find puzzling—the collaborative nature of universities. Not only do we willingly share our preliminary research at conferences, through working papers and peer review; we also share our approaches to teaching, budgeting, administration, etc."[36]

Faculty are demotivated when they see roadblocks placed in the way of doing their work. Often university administrators (gulp) are blamed for these barriers: the class size or the classroom is too big or too small, they cannot get funding for a promising new academic program, there are not enough doctoral student to help with research, and so on. Faculty believe that what they are researching and teaching is incredibly important, even irreplaceable, and it is in the university's best interest that they hold these strong beliefs. Passion goes a long way. While faculty understand at some level the concept of limited resources, the compromises that these limits impose on their work are difficult for them to accept. This is particularly true when faculty are presented obstacles in the guise of a business-oriented practice, for example, a new approach to university budgeting or staffing. If the term "corporatization" gets mentioned, this is not a compliment. Faculty see this as yet another way in which bureaucracy challenges their profession.

In conclusion, faculty spend many years working long hours with often uncertain outcomes to get where they are. They want to be recognized and paid fairly for the work they have chosen, and they want the necessary resources to do it well. When put this way, faculty are not so different from people in business or any other sector of American society.

Organization, Affiliation, and Influence inside the University

Academic institutions may look hierarchical on an organizational chart but they have many centers of power. —David Perlmutter

None of the people you think are in charge are actually in charge. —Business executive and university board chair

In previous chapters, we touched on a number of points related to how influence operates in colleges and universities. We showed that a great deal of what goes on inside universities—including admissions policies, student disciplinary procedures, handling reports of sexual abuse, and free speech policies—is influenced by forces outside universities. Budgets, tuition, and decisions to create or terminate programs are subject to legislatures in public universities and to boards in both public and private institutions. Even academic matters are shaped by outside influences, especially those that relate to accreditation standards, which operate with the remote but serious threat of federal government denial of financial aid.[1]

We also noted that the academic chain of command is much less definitive than in most businesses, so it is rare for specific directions to be passed down through the organizational hierarchy. In particular, university presidents and provosts seldom give orders to deans, who in turn rarely give orders to department heads. As Robert Gates concluded in comparing his roles in various sectors, "At the CIA and Defense I supposedly could tell people what to do, whereas persuasion was my only recourse at [Texas] A&M."[2] Along similar lines, Scott Beardsley, who came to academic leadership from McKinsey & Company Global Management Consulting, concluded that "[academic] leaders must operate and succeed in . . . complex environments that include the various power brokers involved in shared governance."[3]

We additionally have mentioned how faculty see their professional

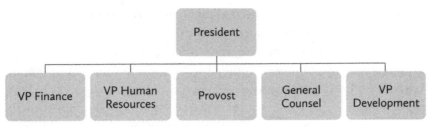

6.1. Generic university organization chart.

standards and judgment as the most important guarantors of quality, with intervention from above seen as largely counterproductive. As we discussed in the introduction, the closest that colleges come to a bottom line is the pursuit of prestige or reputation. Faculty (and specifically the quality of the faculty) in large part determine the reputation of the institution. We've also looked at the division of faculty loyalties between their academic fields and their university (often tilted toward the former). Considering each of these unique characteristics of faculty within the university helps us to better understand the inner workings of academic organizations.

In this chapter, we explore the organization and affiliation of university leaders as well as how influence among them operates. Let's begin with a typical organization chart for the top levels of a university (see figure 6.1). As we have mentioned previously, at this level the university operates much like a business of similar size. The president (sometimes called the chancellor) has overall responsibility for the institution's performance and is expected to establish a vision or direction for the institution to pursue. The president's authority is delegated from the board, which generally has sole legal authority to govern the university.[4] The president works with the board (and in public universities, the legislature) and other constituencies to promote the organization's success and reputation. Whatever academic affiliation the president may have had is likely a distant memory, although it is probably reflected in a deeper understanding of some parts of the university. Presidents in recent years have been criticized for operating (and being compensated) like business chief executive officers. Whatever the validity of this criticism, it is certainly true that the role of university president has grown in scope and complexity to rival the roles of corporate CEOs.

The leaders who report to the president (which may also include vice presidents of information technology, communications, and diversity, as well the director of athletics and the head of the hospital, if the university has one) are experienced individuals with deep expertise in their particular areas. They likely have many direct reports of their own and sizable staffs, with whom they interact in a businesslike manner. With the exception of the provost, these individuals are unlikely to have PhDs, and many people in these roles have spent considerable time in business or professional organizations. The hiring process at this level is similar to that of a business and often involves search consultants and committees.

This group of leaders may have a name such as the senior leadership team or the president's cabinet. They meet on a recurrent basis, and the president also meets regularly with each individual leader. They are expected to keep the president and one another apprised of developments in their respective areas. Further, they are expected to and generally do take a pan-university perspective. Presidents often strive for consensus among this group when making major decisions but will operate without consensus when necessary.

The differences at this organizational level relative to businesses are largely those we have already discussed: the absence of an overarching goal like profit, a strong sense of ownership and responsibility for the institution's reputation, the need to reconcile often dramatically different expectations of stakeholder groups (including the board), and a very long time horizon. An experienced board member recently told us that leading a university is "more like running a country with several branches of government than running a business." For this reason, even if most senior university leaders have business backgrounds, decisions take longer than in business settings. As Jim Collins put it, "Social sector [including university] leaders are not less decisive than business leaders as a general rule; they only appear that way to those who fail to grasp the complex governance and diffuse power structures common to social sectors."[5]

In a private business, many of the senior executives will have spent their careers in the same industry if not the same company, but this is often not the case in academics. One senior leadership team we know is made up of people who came from two different law firms, a private equity firm, several universities and academic disciplines, a government agency, a public relations firm, and a professional sports team. With such diverse backgrounds, expectations for how the team should operate vary widely and need to be managed toward at least a rough

6.2. Generic academic organization chart.

consensus. Otherwise, everything is negotiable, including what constitutes a crisis, who is involved in which issues, which constituencies matter most (and when this balance changes), whose vote counts, and how decisions will be made and communicated.

It is within the academic component (see figure 6.2) that colleges and universities operate much differently from businesses, much to the consternation, and sometimes confusion, of businesspeople who are associated with them in one way or another. What is going on? How and why is it so different?[6]

Provost

The provost often is referred to as the chief academic officer (or CAO) and often is seen as first among equals of the direct reports to the president or chancellor. He or she has overall responsibility for education and research within and throughout the institution. Provosts often have a considerable number of direct reports (more than twenty in large universities), including deans, vice provosts, the university librarian, and sometimes even heads of functions such as human resources, information technology, and student affairs. In some settings, the provost operates as a kind of chief operating officer, leading the institution from the inside, while the president focuses outwardly on fund-raising and external relations. Robert Hendrickson and his colleagues point out, "For this working relationship to be successful, the president must give the CAO space to perform his or her role and responsibilities and not micromanage."[7]

Whatever their academic background (most have been deans), provosts must take on a pan-university perspective and have to learn quickly about the variety of academic disciplines and other functions that report to them. Provosts often also have significant budgetary responsibility, so they must learn how to lead the budget process. They quickly find that they will constantly be lobbied to support various initiatives. As Howard Aldrich and Solvi Lillejord point out, provosts and other academic leaders (especially new ones) are unusually dependent for information on the people to whom they allocate resources.[8] This is partly due to the low level of support staffing and IT resources relative to comparable positions in private businesses.

One of the ways in which provosts exert influence on deans and faculty is by offering funding for research or teaching enhancements. The provost's challenge is to reward people who make the institution better without appearing to play favorites. The solution is to fund initiatives that best meet a set of objective criteria and to have a representative group of senior faculty make the funding decisions. As John Lombardi wisely indicates, creating financial incentives for desired behavior will generally be more effective than putting forward strategic plans or mission statements.[9]

Deans

Like heads of business units in a multi-business firm, deans have overall responsibility for their respective units and generally enjoy a great deal of independence, especially when they have been in place for some time and their schools are self-supporting.[10] Like presidents, they are expected to articulate a vision or direction for their college or school. Their direct reports include associate deans and department heads (who in larger institutions report to associate deans). Deans of larger schools may also have a staff infrastructure (IT, HR, and fundraising). Deans generally are hired—from either inside or outside the institution—by a thorough search process usually involving faculty and often involving search firms and committees. They are almost always drawn from the academic or professional community represented by their college or school. They can be chemistry or sociology professors or lawyers or dentists. They are much more knowledgeable about their professions and schools than about generic higher education issues. However, the dean of the College of Arts and Sciences (by whatever name[s]) has the most diverse set of areas under his or her responsibility and will be challenged to understand them at a level that will satisfy the faculty.

Deans represent the line of demarcation between a pan-university affiliation and one focused on a specific school. While deans contribute to the overall institution, their aspirations, goals, and performance measurements are focused on their units. Moreover, faculty *expect* their deans to advocate for their schools with university administration in matters of budget and staffing and hold them accountable for doing so in the dean's review process. While provosts and vice presidents live their day-to-day lives surrounded by information about higher education issues and the overall performance of their institutions, deans are immersed in information about their particular schools and professions. For example, business school deans are much more likely to read *Harvard Business Review* or academic journals such as the *Journal of Finance* than the *Chronicle of Higher Education*.[11]

Deans often realize early in their tenure, to their chagrin, that they effectively have no one to implement their agenda. We have seen several deans experienced in business but not in academics who quickly came to this realization. The faculty, including department chairs, are preoccupied with their teaching and research and the specific needs of their departments. The dean can more easily shape the time and attention of the staff, but there are few important initiatives in academics that can be implemented solely by staff.

This reality leaves deans with several options. They can hire external consultants to study an issue and then promote the solution to the faculty. This approach brings useful expertise to the issue but will arouse faculty suspicion that the consultants are doing the dean's bidding and shortchanging the faculty perspective. Or deans can create new staff positions, adding a quasi-permanent new cost while still limiting the involvement of faculty. They also can create (drumroll, eye roll) a faculty committee or task force. These groups promote faculty buy-in but may take a (very) long time, and the faculty may or may not have the expertise or incentive to complete the task. Finally, a hybrid approach is for the dean to appoint a faculty member as head of the initiative: someone responsible for both gathering the necessary expertise and mobilizing the necessary faculty support. This strategy works well if the dean can pull it off, but it is challenging because the kind of respected faculty members needed to spearhead an initiative often drive an expensive bargain to be pulled away from their academic work.

Department Heads

Department heads, sometimes called department chairs, are responsible for teaching and research in a specific academic area. They may be chosen by the dean or associate dean or elected by the faculty in their department. Often the senior faculty in a department reluctantly take turns over a period of years serving as department head. This generally is not a job that faculty are passionate about taking on, unless they have aspirations for going to the "dark side," that is, becoming full-time university administrators.[12] The reluctance of faculty to assume even first-level leadership opportunities within their own department, let alone higher-level positions in the university, is another fundamental difference between academic and business organizations.

There is little question about the affiliation of department heads: they represent their colleagues and their academic discipline, especially when they are rotating through the position as a form of service. However, they are expected by deans and associate deans to be responsible citizens and to some extent become leaders of the college or school. This expectation gives rise to the central tension in the lives of department heads: the need to represent their colleagues and their discipline to university administration but also to represent the administration to their colleagues. We are reminded of a classic description of first-level supervisors as "master and victim of double talk."[13] One department head we know was criticized by the administration for being too department-centric in handling a specific issue and simultaneously criticized by departmental colleagues for bowing to the administration in handling the same issue.

It is no wonder faculty do not line up to take these departmental leadership positions. Senior administrators view department heads with some justification as volunteers, and thus they are reluctant to be overly critical of them. Without a deep bench of people who want the position, department heads' credible threat to quit and go back to what they love is an important source of upward influence, as well as a limit on downward influence. It is difficult to find a similar situation in business.

While the figures and explanations above may create the impression that these organizational dynamics, affiliation, and influence are mostly similar to businesses but with some quirks, the next two sections provide a counterpoint, explaining some ways in which the two types of organizations—businesses and universities—differ even more profoundly.

Faculty Governance

The concept of faculty governance (or shared governance) signifies that influence over colleges and university organizational decision-making is shared between faculty and the administration and that certain decisions are the sole province of the faculty.[14] The concept dates to principles put forward in 1920 and refined in 1940 by the American Association of University Professors and elaborated in a third statement signed in 1966 not only by the AAUP but also by the Association of Governing Boards and the American Council on Education.[15] This means that organizations representing faculty, boards, and college presidents all signed this statement, certainly indicating broad agreement in principle. Perhaps this level of accord was possible because what was agreed upon was indeed a set of principles as opposed to a binding set of specific terms. Indeed, exactly what is meant by faculty governance is open to interpretation.[16] Despite (or because of) this ambiguity, the AAUP sometimes steps in to sanction institutions for "substantial non-compliance."[17]

The role of faculty governance proposed in the 1966 statement is quite broad. While many people equate faculty governance with the faculty senate, the AAUP's foundational statement on this concept is much more expansive. The following excerpts illustrate its intent:[18]

> The faculty has primary responsibility for such fundamental areas as curriculum, subject matter and methods of instruction, research, faculty status, and those aspects of student life which relate to the educational process. On those matters the power of review or final decision lodged in the governing board or delegated by it to the president should be exercised adversely only in exceptional circumstances.
>
> The faculty sets the requirements for the degrees offered in course, determines when the requirements have been met, and authorizes the president and board to grant the degrees thus achieved.
>
> Faculty status and related matters are primarily a faculty responsibility; this area includes appointments, reappointments,

decisions not to reappoint, promotions, the granting of tenure, and dismissal.... Furthermore, scholars in a particular field or activity have the chief competence for judging the work of their colleagues....

The faculty should actively participate in the determination of policies and procedures governing salary increases....

Agencies for faculty participation in the government of the college or university should be established at each level where faculty responsibility is present.

In their 2003 study, William Tierney and James T. Minor identified three general approaches used by academic institutions to implement the AAUP concept of university shared governance:

1. Fully collaborative decision-making: organizational decisions are shared among faculty and administration.
2. Consultative decision-making: the administration and the board retain authority but consult with faculty.
3. Distributive decision-making: decisions are delegated to the board, administration, or faculty based on previous agreement.

Tierney and Minor indicate that colleges and universities also use other methods to implement faculty governance, including the decision-making rights of academic departments and the presence of governing units at the school level.[19]

Whatever the precise mechanisms, the overall thrust of shared governance is a significant level of faculty involvement in decision-making on academic matters. This concept is broadly illustrated in figure 6.3, in which two equally powerful entities—faculty and administration—share influence over university decisions. Some areas fall within the bailiwick of the administration (such as the budget), some are shared (for example, the appointment of deans), and some are under the responsibilities of the faculty (such as the curriculum). This depiction can be contrasted with figures 6.1 and 6.2 as rival concepts of how influence operates in academic institutions. In this comparison, the organization charts in these earlier figures would fit within the circle on the left. The bottom line here is that business-oriented concepts of organization and influence tell only part of the story of how academic institutions operate.

Shared governance is often made concrete by campus-level policies

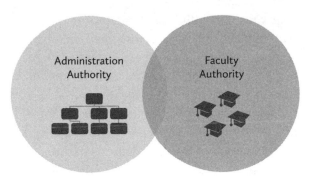

6.3. Shared governance.

Administration
Authority

Faculty
Authority

and traditions for how specific institutional decisions are made. For example, the selection of a dean frequently is shaped by a faculty selection committee (appointed by the provost), which provides the provost with the names of several acceptable candidates, with the final selection and negotiation done by the provost, who is ultimately accountable for the success of the choice.[20] Many deans at UNC–Chapel Hill have been hired via this method, which is used at numerous institutions to choose new provosts and even presidents. Boards or administrators who make such important personnel decisions without faculty consultation risk strong blowback and negative repercussions from the standpoint of shared governance.[21]

The faculty senate, which represents the faculty in policy development and decision-making, is the most visible symbol of institutional commitment to shared governance. Its members and leadership team are elected by the faculty, and, especially in larger institutions, much of the work is done in its committees.[22] UNC–Chapel Hill has a faculty council, while the University of Wisconsin–Eau Claire has a university senate (whose authority is supported by a Wisconsin state statute).[23] Like many smaller institutions, the Pomona College faculty operate as a committee of the whole, with a chair of the faculty and an executive committee.[24] Gonzaga has both a faculty assembly made up of all faculty and an elected faculty senate.[25] The Air Force Academy has an academy board comprised of both faculty and nonfaculty, with several standing committees.[26] Finally, Carnegie Mellon has a faculty organization (all faculty) and an elected faculty senate, whose statement captures the understanding of many faculty of the purpose of this body:

> In accordance with normal practice at major institutions of higher education in the United States, the professionals constituting

the faculty bear a primary responsibility for all matters of educational and research policy and of academic freedom. As a means of discharging this responsibility, a chief purpose of the Faculty Organization is to examine these matters and formulate recommendations to the president and other appropriate persons. With a view to the institution's continued success and improvement, the Faculty Organization also has the prerogative of considering any other topic relevant to the interests of the university as well as any topic affecting the welfare of the university community, and to make recommendations thereon.... The representative assembly of the Faculty Organization is the Faculty Senate.[27]

In reflecting on his time as president of Texas A&M, Robert Gates strongly advocates collaboration with the faculty senate: "While faculty are, by nature, independent actors who are rarely motivated en masse, there are faculty organizations that can play an important and constructive role. I worked hard to develop close, cooperative relationships with each of these groups, and the effort paid off with the faculty as a whole in gaining their support for what I was trying to accomplish."[28]

Finding a business analogue to the concept of shared governance as exemplified by the faculty senate is difficult, but one might be European Works Councils. Although these legally mandated bodies operate in the context of multinational businesses and unionized employees, the practice of an organization's leadership collaborating with the people responsible for its core work processes is at least in spirit similar to shared governance.[29] American labor unions are not an apt comparison to shared governance, as their influence is generally limited to salary negotiations and rules about seniority. Also, both college administrators and faculty have some expectation of collaboration on important decisions, which is absent in unionized industries.

Is Faculty Governance in Decline?

A number of observers have noted that shared governance practices are increasingly failing to provide the appropriate level of faculty influence in college and university decision-making. Higher education journalist Goldie Blumenstyk says that some faculty believe that "decisions that once fell under the purview of 'shared governance' ... are

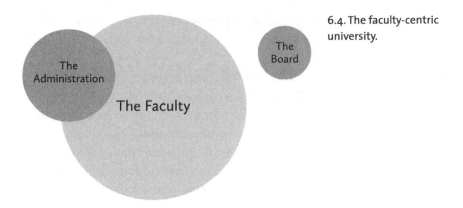

6.4. The faculty-centric university.

now being handled by administrators, or that the consultation is more *pro forma* than genuine."[30] Gates writes, "Faculty are deeply suspicious of university administrators and their often empty promises of 'shared governance.'"[31]

Reasons for this mistrust include the increasing number of non-tenure-track faculty in colleges and universities, who are sometimes excluded from faculty governance (often by the tenured faculty themselves).[32] Author and university professor Larry Gerber argues that the rise of adjunct faculty and an increasingly corporate style of management, combined with the reluctance of faculty members under performance pressure to participate in governance activities, have weakened the system of shared governance over several decades. Gerber believes that this trend represents a threat to the quality of American higher education.[33] His concerns, and those of faculty at many institutions, are echoed by political scientist Benjamin Ginsberg, who like Gerber asserts that the success of American colleges and universities is founded on faculty influence and that its erosion is deeply problematic.[34]

The Faculty-Centric University

Many faculty have an implicit view of academic organizations, depicted in figure 6.4, which represents a profound challenge to the hierarchical organization chart model in figures 6.1 and 6.2. It is this view that leads board members and other business professionals, when they encounter it in academic institutions, to wonder what planet they have landed on. From this perspective, the faculty more or less *are* the university.[35] They recognize the existence of such entities as administration and boards, but these groups are understood to be clearly ancillary to the faculty.[36] Everything in figures 6.1 and 6.2 shrinks further into the small circle on the left.

Lest this depiction seem extreme and perhaps even untrue as a representation of faculty thinking, consider the following story from Gary A. Olson in the *Chronicle of Higher Education*: "A dean [reported] that a faculty leader at her institution told her that ... professors, who are the 'heart of the university,' delegate the governance of their universities to administrators, whose role is to provide a support network for the faculty. 'He said, in all seriousness, that faculty have the primary role of governing the university and that administrators are appointed to spare them from the more distasteful managerial labor,' said the dean with incredulity."[37]

This scenario shows both the pure view of the faculty-centric university and the amazement, at least of one administrator, upon seeing it in its unvarnished and unabashed form. Or consider this statement from Ginsberg, which we have to admit is pretty entertaining: "Generally speaking, a million-dollar president could be kidnapped by space aliens and it would be weeks or even months before his or her absence from campus was noticed."[38]

In the faculty-centric view, all important work is done by the faculty. We discussed in chapter 5 how faculty see their teaching and research as overwhelmingly important to the institution. We now can add that many faculty see the work done by administration as inconsequential, which is good news in case space aliens actually do invade. Faculty know that universities were founded by scholars and that administrators as we understand them today—and especially in such large numbers—are a recent phenomenon. While Benjamin Whorf's famous hypothesis about the relationship between language and cognition (remember how many words Eskimos have for snow?) has often been misunderstood, the fact that faculty refer to presidents, provosts, and deans as administrators, as opposed to leaders or even managers, tells us something about their views.[39]

Recognizing this faculty-centric perspective helps a number of other aspects of higher education organization make more sense. For example, it is not surprising that most faculty do not want to be promoted into administration. They hardly see it as a promotion; instead it means trading valuable work for work that at best is a necessary evil. After all, if the university is essentially a community of scholars, what role of any importance could administrators play? Answer: to ensure generous funding for my unit and to handle all nonacademic responsibilities without me having to be involved.

We have two final points to make before we move on. One, administrators make more decisions than faculty think they should because the faculty are focused on their research and teaching while administrators spend virtually all of their time working on administrative issues. And two, faculty views of the power of university administrators vary significantly across the institution. When we were charged with implementing government-mandated Title IX training, it was striking how uncontroversial it was in the professional schools, especially medicine, where faculty were accustomed to rules (such as HIPAA) and a more hierarchical approach. The arts and humanities faculty were, however, reluctant, and many simply ignored the requirement, at least initially. We moved cautiously in dealing with them because we had been advised by a sage colleague at another university (who will not be outed here), "Don't pick a fight with the humanities faculty. They have a lot of time on their hands and they write really well."

7 What Is Academic Research?

Research is another area where there is a significant gulf in understanding between those inside and those outside higher education. In this chapter, we explain some of the most basic and important issues regarding academic research, including research methods, funding, modes of publication and assessment, and commercialization.[1]

Many university mission statements focus on the creation and dissemination of new knowledge. Research is the process of creating new knowledge, while publication, teaching, and commercialization are the primary methods for its dissemination.

In research-intensive universities (see chapter 2), most tenure-track faculty spend a significant amount of time on their research. What exactly are they doing? It is hard to give a simple answer to this question, as the nature of research differs dramatically across academic disciplines. Here are a few representative examples:

- Professors from the medical and pharmacy schools are trying to determine whether a new drug is more effective than an existing drug in treating a disease. This research project started in a laboratory, progressed through animal testing, and will conclude with the study of patients with the disease in question. Conducting this research involves a multiyear process of designing the studies, securing human subject approvals, and collecting and analyzing data. It will likely involve collaboration with a contract research organization to conduct clinical trials as well as with a hospital system to identify patients to serve as research subjects. This example suggests an important point about biomedical research: that it is often done in interdisciplinary teams rather than by individuals. The outcome of this research could be the introduction of a new and more effective drug to treat the disease, but many things have to go right for this to happen.

- Professors in the business school and sociology department are trying to understand the factors that contribute to successful entrepreneurship. They use a variety of methods, including review of public databases on the formation, growth, and closing of businesses, as well as surveys of and interviews with entrepreneurs. The culmination of this research will be a quantitative model of successful entrepreneurship, the predictive power of which will be assessed using multivariate statistics. The outcome of this research could be a better understanding of entrepreneurship that would guide public policy, investment decisions, and the decisions of entrepreneurs.

- An English professor is interested in understanding the evolution of a particular theme in the plays of Shakespeare.[2] She diligently and repeatedly reads the plays themselves, of course, which likely involves analyzing different editions of the same play. The editions may be in several different libraries and may or may not be available electronically. She also will review, with great interest and intensity, the existing literature on Shakespeare, which is, to say the least, massive (a Google search gives 60 *million* results, but Google Scholar narrows it to only 1.4 million).[3] She may decide on a new theoretical perspective to understand and critique Shakespeare's work. For example, she may use contemporary theories of race to explore the dynamics among Othello, Iago, and Desdemona. The findings can help scholars and students understand Shakespeare's developing views about multiracial relationships and how they are expressed in his subsequent works.[4]

There are many additional types of research we could have mentioned. For example, some scientific research is more fundamental than the pharmacy research mentioned above. Scientists may investigate the basic structure of certain molecules, which could lead to new pharmaceutical substances in a number of years. This research is often referred to as "basic," which unfortunately leads some people to understand it as "elementary," when the actual meaning is "fundamental."[5] It is important to understand that research project teams may comprise faculty, postdoctoral fellows, graduate and undergraduate students, and technical staff.

For some faculty in arts-oriented departments, creative artistic activity takes the place of research. For example, new ideas may be expressed via a painting, a sculpture, a live musical performance, or a recording. Increasingly, such creative activity takes a digital form.

Why Do Faculty Do Research?

These examples suggest the vast differences in the activities included in the term "research." We are tempted here to mention that academics cannot even agree on how to pronounce the word, with some favoring REsearch, others reSEARCH. Tomato, tomahto. But whatever the research questions and methods, and however the word is pronounced, there are a number of reasons why faculty conduct research.

Based on our discussion in chapter 5, one obvious reason faculty engage in research is to earn promotion and tenure. For tenure-track faculty in research universities, this requirement is nonnegotiable. Most faculty are achievement-oriented; they were among the best students at each stage of their education. So, it is not surprising that they continue the quest for achievement through the various levels of academic promotion and tenure. But as our earlier discussion suggested, many faculty members have a deep passion for what they are studying. Whether it is finding a better cure for a disease, a better understanding of entrepreneurship, or new insights into Shakespeare, faculty consider their research as among the defining elements of their lives, and not just their professional lives. Even after they have received all of the promotions they are ever going to receive, they will still work long hours and go to extraordinary lengths to pursue their research. For readers who have studied organizational behavior and recall the term "intrinsic motivation," this is it.

Another reason faculty conduct research is to earn a position of respect within their academic discipline (including their home department). Remember that academic communities, formed around specific disciplines such as chemistry, sociology, economics, computer science, and philosophy, transcend individual universities and often are more important to faculty than their own institutions. Faculty's reputational status in the academic community is derived from successful research and publication. Status conveys a number of benefits beyond the significant psychological benefits to those who have it. It will lead to invitations to join the boards of the leading journals in the field, which further enhances one's reputation. It also likely will lead to job offers at prestigious universities, which again increases one's status, even if the offers are not accepted. A strong reputation helps faculty to attract the most promising graduate students, first to their university and second to their own research projects (from among the students who have already been accepted). Finally, high levels of academic status are rewarded, albeit imperfectly, with higher pay. This brings us to the question of who pays for the research that confers these benefits to faculty.

How Is Research Funded?

The likelihood of external funding (funding from outside the institution) for research parallels our three examples. While it differs among fields in each category, external funding is highest for research in medicine and the natural sciences, medium in the social sciences, and lowest in the arts and humanities. It is important to note that much research in many disciplines does not receive any external funding. Colleges and universities often provide small amounts of funding to cover incidental costs of research (travel, research assistance, and the like), especially for faculty early in their career. In research universities, faculty teaching responsibilities are designed to allow for time to be spent on research. If we recognize faculty members' time as a cost of research (and in some disciplines, it is the largest cost), it is fair to say that research universities subsidize research through teaching loads lower (and in some cases much lower) than in colleges and universities where teaching is the sole focus for faculty.

Research in medicine and the sciences (including social science) may be funded by one of two large government agencies, the National Institutes of Health and the National Science Foundation. Other elements of the federal government that support research include the Defense Department, the Department of Education, and the Department of Agriculture. Private foundations and industry also provide significant support for university research.

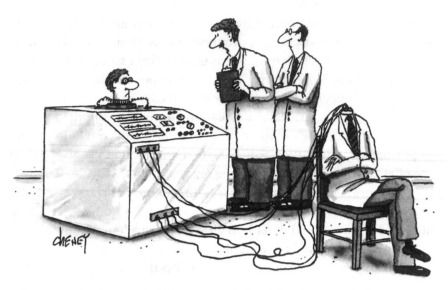

"Bad news, Phil—due to federal funding cutbacks, we can't afford to put your head back on."

7.1. *Source*: Tom Cheney/The New Yorker Collection/The Cartoon Bank.

THE NATIONAL INSTITUTES OF HEALTH

Founded in 1887, the National Institutes of Health now is part of the Department of Health and Human Services. Located near Washington in Bethesda, Maryland, the NIH has an annual budget of about $27 billion and is by far the largest funder of university research in the United States. Its goal is "to acquire new knowledge to help prevent, detect, diagnose, and treat disease and disability, from the rarest genetic disorder to the common cold." Its mission is "to uncover new knowledge that will lead to better health for everyone."[6]

The scope of the NIH is so vast that it is hard to summarize, but research program areas include biotechnology, cancer, genetics, infectious diseases, neuroscience, and women's health. This means that NIH funding is, in principle, available to researchers in a wide range of fields.

Faculty receive support for their research by submitting a grant proposal to a specific NIH program before one of its periodic deadlines.[7] Once proposals have been received, NIH program directors convene a panel of experts in the field who review the proposals and rank them in quality. It is an honor to be invited to these NIH study sections, as they are called, and faculty take this work very seriously. NIH research programs are extremely competitive. The amount of funding available vis-à-vis the number of applications received determines the probability of funding, but in general it is less than 20 percent, and sometimes much lower. It is not uncommon for faculty members to apply for NIH funding several times before being successful, nor is it uncommon for faculty never to be successful in their pursuit of NIH funding.

The NIH's most common type of grant is the Research Project Grant (R01), which is "used to support a discrete, specified, circumscribed research project." The average R01 funding is about $500,000. Many researchers and their labs are supported for years on R01 grants, but they must periodically (at least every five years) compete for this funding. The NIH also provides Research Program Project Grants and Center Core Grants, both of which support large projects by research teams. Also important are training grants, which help to prepare the next generation of scientists.

A small number of universities receive the lion's share of NIH funding. One analysis shows that the top 10 percent of universities receiving NIH grants got 75 percent of the funding.[8] Top NIH-funded institutions include Johns Hopkins University, the University of California at San Francisco, the University of Michigan, the University of Pennsylvania, and the University of Pittsburgh.[9] Having said this, even a small amount of funding can make a huge difference in the ability of faculty to conduct their research.

THE NATIONAL SCIENCE FOUNDATION

The National Science Foundation is younger and smaller than the NIH; it was founded in 1950 and has a research budget of about $6 billion. It is located in Alexandria, Virginia, across the Potomac River from D.C., and its purpose is "to promote the progress of science; to advance the national health, prosperity, and welfare; [and] to secure the national defense."[10] Its scope includes research in biological sciences; computer science; education in science and mathematics; engineering; geosciences; mathematics; physical sciences; and social, behavioral, and economic sciences. The NSF operates in a manner similar to the NIH: programs and deadlines are announced, experts are convened, and funding decisions are made. The probability of success for competitive NSF grants is slightly more than 20 percent. The typical NSF grant is about $150,000, with a term of about three years.[11]

THE NATIONAL ENDOWMENT FOR THE ARTS AND
THE NATIONAL ENDOWMENT FOR THE HUMANITIES

In 1964 President Lyndon Johnson made a speech at Brown University in support of federal funding for the arts and humanities, and in 1965 he signed into law the National Foundation on the Arts and Humanities Act. The law established the National Endowment for the Arts and the National Endowment for the Humanities, separate and independent federal agencies with a combined annual budget of about $300 million. The NEA and the NEH provide grants to cultural institutions such as libraries, museums, colleges, and universities, as well as funding to individuals such as faculty members and researchers. Both funding and leadership for these agencies are controlled by Congress.

Dedicated to "supporting excellence in the arts, both new and established; bringing the arts to all Americans; and providing leadership in arts education,"[12] the NEA notably provides support to tribal colleges and historically black colleges and universities. Further, "it is a principal source, if not the only funding source, for projects promoting folk arts, preserving historical traditions, and providing arts education in rural and low-income communities all over the country."[13]

The NEH "serves and strengthens our Republic by promoting excellence in the humanities and conveying the lessons of history to all Americans. The Endowment accomplishes this mission by providing grants for high-quality humanities projects in four funding areas: preserving and providing access to cultural resources, education, research, and public programs."[14] Faculty in the humanities may also seek NEH support through its fellowship programs.

Despite some political rhetoric in opposition to federal support for the arts and humanities, funding for the NEA[15] and the NEH has remained constant for the past two decades.[16] There is expanding evidence that "educational programs that mutually integrate learning experiences in the humanities, arts, and STEM lead to improved educational and career outcomes for undergraduate and graduate students."[17]

PRIVATE FOUNDATIONS

Research funding also comes from private foundations. Some of the most important of these are the Bill and Melinda Gates Foundation, the Howard Hughes Medical Institute, the Chan Zuckerberg Initiative, the Alfred P. Sloan Foundation, and the Andrew W. Mellon Foundation. With the exception of the Gates Foundation (annual support of about $5 billion), these foundations are much smaller than the NSF. However, as funding available from private foundations increases and funding from government organizations remains flat, the overall share of research funded by private sources (including corporations) has increased substantially over the past few years.[18] Each private foundation has a unique set of research priorities, but collectively they fund a wide range of research.

OVERHEAD PAYMENTS

Universities in which significant research is conducted maintain a substantial infrastructure to support it, including facilities (such as laboratories), instruments, ventilation equipment, spaces to keep animals, and people who ensure regulatory compliance, conduct financial analysis, and file reports, among many other activities. In recognition of these requirements, government funding agencies support not only the direct costs of research but also the indirect costs—that is, overhead. This infrastructure support, generally known as facilities and administrative costs (or F&A), is a major means of support for colleges and universities from the federal government. The F&A or indirect cost rate paid by government agencies to universities is negotiated based on a periodic cost study conducted by the government. Once the rate is established, it is paid, at least in principle, by all government agencies. The range of F&A, expressed as a percentage of direct costs, is roughly 50 to 60 percent and is generally higher at private institutions.[19] Private foundations generally pay a much lower overhead rate, and some pay none at all.[20]

There is a perception in some quarters that F&A operates as a sort of slush fund at academic institutions that receive it, but this is not an accurate characterization. The overhead funding provided by government agencies is based on a detailed audit of actual facility and administrative costs, conducted by government agencies whose interest is to limit their assessment of these costs. Furthermore, reimbursement for documented administrative costs is limited by government policy, which means that universities are likely to pay a meaningful share of their own infrastructure costs, whatever their reimbursement rate. Research is a crucially important business for universities to be in, but it is not a profitable business. In fact, the aggressive pursuit of funded research despite this fact is further evidence that universities focus on mission and reputation over financial gain.

Finally, readers may wonder who within the university actually receives the reimbursement for indirect costs. The answer is different at each university. The distribution formula for reimbursements from indirect costs is the outcome of extensive policy development and negotiation processes, with funds often shared among the principal investigator, his or her academic department, the school or college, and the overall university. F&A goes to cover real costs incurred by the university to support research, but generally no one in the mix believes that he or she is getting a fair share.

How Is Research Published?

Academic journals constitute the most common method for publishing university research. One recent study estimated that there are nearly 30,000 English-language journals, and that number continues to grow.[21] Researchers preparing to submit their work for publication in a journal first will circulate it among colleagues for feedback and make a number of revisions before submission in yet another example of the significant role played by the academic communities that span colleges and universities.

Academic journals have careful standardized processes to review submitted manuscripts. They use members of their editorial boards (composed of distinguished researchers) as well as ad hoc reviewers to review manuscripts; this is known as the peer review process. As we discussed in chapter 5, faculty relate to and identify with colleagues within their own discipline more so than with faculty in different disciplines at their own institutions. Thus, peer review provides legitimacy and objectivity to the evaluation of research and new knowledge. Peers, also known as referees, evaluate the quality of research submitted as journal articles, books, or grant proposals. Peer review also is crucial to evaluating the body of a faculty member's work at the time of promotion and tenure; department colleagues weighing in on those decisions rely heavily upon the expert opinions provide by peer experts within the same discipline.

Once the reviewers (most often two to three) have submitted their reviews, the editor or associate editor of the journal makes a decision about whether to publish the manuscript. The most common decision is outright rejection, especially in the most prestigious journals, which publish only a tiny fraction of the manuscripts they receive. The other common outcome is the request for revision, also known as revise and resubmit, or R&R. When researchers receive this outcome, they go back to work on the manuscript, attempting to revise it in a manner that will satisfy the reviewers and editor and will result in publication.[22]

When the authors resubmit a manuscript, it goes back to either the same or different reviewers, who again review the paper and send reviews to the editor. The most common outcomes are still rejection and R&R, but with two new possibilities: conditional acceptance or outright acceptance. The former often means acceptance in principle, but with some very clear revisions to be made. The latter means a celebration for the authors. The R&R process may be repeated several times before either the paper is accepted or the authors give up. The impact on faculty morale of acceptance versus rejection is analogous to the impact on an attorney who wins or loses a big case or on a senior consultant who wins or loses a major potential engagement.[23]

Journals, like academic institutions, can be described as more or less prestigious, and faculty strive to have their research published in the most prestigious journals. Often there are only a few journals in a field that are seen as appropriate outlets for research, especially at elite institutions.[24] In general, professors will submit their research to the most prestigious journal where they believe they have a reasonable chance of acceptance. If the paper does not get accepted there, they will move down the prestige scale to another journal and if necessary to another, often taking years of time. This means that, with requests for revisions, they will rewrite their paper many times. By the time a paper is published, the author most likely is sick of it. It is also worth mentioning that academic worlds can be very small. If authors decide to change journals rather than to try to meet reviewer demands, they may get the same reviewers at the new journal.

The other major way in which academics attempt to publish their work is, of course, books. The prevalence of books for publishing academic research in different fields is roughly the inverse of the likelihood of research funding: it is highest in the arts and humanities, medium in the social sciences, and lowest in the natural sciences and medicine. Many academic books are issued by publishing houses associated with universities, with a status hierarchy roughly corresponding to that of their affiliated universities, which may or may not own them. Academic publishers use a review process similar to the journal review process, so faculty who publish with them can rightly claim that their books were subjected to peer review.

Before leaving this topic, readers should know that the economic models for both types of publishing are under pressure. Journal subscription costs are high, and journal publishers generally offer journals in packages ("bundles") that universities feel that they cannot refuse to purchase. This has led to attempts by universities to claim their intellectual property and to put the published work of their faculty into an electronic repository for open access, so that scholars can access it even if they or their institutions cannot afford to subscribe to the journals. Regarding book publishing, academic libraries must be increasingly selective about which books they can buy, partly due to flat or declining funding and partly due to high journal costs. This puts the publication of academic books at risk. Institutions are considering a range of solutions to these issues, which as of this writing are far from resolved.[25]

How Is Research Evaluated?

We discussed in chapter 5 a number of times in faculty members' careers when their research is evaluated. Examples include when they apply for a first or any subsequent academic job, when they are considered for promotion and tenure, and when they are reviewed in the posttenure review process. What is the basis for this evaluation? The process and evidence used vary from one university to the next and from one academic discipline to the next, but we can provide an idea of the factors most often used to assess academic research.

At the heart of differences in research assessment processes are two related questions. First, is the assessment a matter primarily of peer judgment or of metrics? And second, can the research be validly assessed only by experts in the researcher's field, or by any informed observer? Not surprisingly, the answers to these questions by people in and around universities fall into two patterns: either research must be assessed by expert judgment (perhaps informed by metrics), or it can be assessed by nonexperts using metrics alone.[26] Most university assessment processes are a blend of both approaches, with peer judgment perhaps playing a bigger role at the department level and metrics playing a bigger role at the college or university level. As pressures for accountability mount, the use of metrics for evaluation has significantly increased.[27]

In fields where external funding is available, success in securing funding is a key metric for evaluating a faculty member's research performance. If one is a board member or senior administrator, it is important to understand this process, especially if one is involved in the assessment of that performance. In some fields, the presence or absence of an NIH Ro1 grant is particularly important, especially for promotion and tenure. Note that this is a judgment (of the value of the research by the grant reviewers) wrapped inside a metric (the grant or grants awarded). Of course, in some fields, it is virtually impossible to perform credible research without external funding, due to the intrinsic costs of the research.[28]

Many nonacademics are familiar with the phrase "publish or perish." But how is this principle implemented in evaluations of faculty research? We discuss several possibilities, from the simplest to the most complex, and we focus on fields where research journals are the dominant publication method. The simplest approach is simply to count publications—for example, a researcher needs to have x publications (where x could be almost any number, depending on the field) to be hired/promoted/tenured. The weakness of this approach lies in its oversimplicity, which becomes apparent as we consider the other research evaluation approaches.

As we have discussed, journals can be ordered in terms of their prestige, and prestige in higher education is a very important goal. Simply counting publications equally in all journals ignores these facts, and this approach represents a weak methodology for evaluating the quality of a professor's published research. Some departments address this weakness by doing a weighted count, in which publications in more prestigious journals (sometimes called A journals) count more than those in less prestigious journals (B or C). A simpler alternative to this method is to establish a list of journals that matter; publications not on this list simply do not count at all. Sometimes journals are assigned to categories based on their impact factors, a measure of how much the research published in each journal influences the overall academic field.

Two other approaches are used to assess the impact of research publications: citation analysis and the Hirsch index. Academic works always cite other academic works. One way to assess the quality or impact of a publication is to consider its accumulated citation count, that

is, how often it has been cited in other publications. The reasoning behind this approach is that research is meant to influence the thinking
in one's field. Papers citing a professor's research is evidence of that
professor's influence, and thus his or her prestige, in the field. The primary tools used to assess citations are Google Scholar and the Web of
Science. A promotion and tenure review letter may mention how many
times a researcher's work has been cited. Most academic papers are
cited very few times, and many not at all. If you are new to this and
curious about how it works, search Google Scholar and then insert the
name of a professor to see how often each of his or her papers has been
cited.

A metric that combines the simple count as well as citation analysis
is the Hirsch (or H) index. The H index indicates the number of papers
published by an author that have been cited at least the same number
of times as the number of papers. An H index of ten means that the author has ten papers that have been cited at least ten times each.[29] This
measure combines a lot of information into one number. For a variety
of reasons, the H index is better at comparing scholars within a field as
opposed to scholars in different fields.[30]

The inherent complexity of assessing research[31] reminds us of the famous Churchill quote describing Russia as "a riddle wrapped in a mys-
tery inside an enigma." In fairness, the ambiguity is most pronounced
in the middle of the research performance distribution; agreement
about the most and least successful researchers is easier to determine.
The bottom line is that most academics in a position to make decisions
will consider all available research evaluation metrics, but ultimately
they will use their own expertise and professional judgment to make
sense of the overall picture.

These issues are not, if you will forgive the term, purely academic.
While we were writing this chapter, one of us attended a school-level
promotion and tenure meeting, at which virtually every method we
have identified for assessing research performance was invoked. The
other of us attended an interdepartmental research colloquium where
findings were evaluated based solely on various journal ratings. As we
discussed in chapter 5, the consequences of these decisions are significant for both individual faculty and for the institution.

How Is Research Commercialized?

Commercialization is, like teaching and publication, a means of disseminating knowledge. The commercialization of research is a complex topic that deserves and has received book-length treatment; we will cover only the most fundamental points here. Readers who want a deeper look at commercialization of university research should see Holden Thorp and Buck Goldstein's *Engines of Innovation* or Don Rose and Cam Patterson's *Research to Revenue*.[32] This section draws on both books.

In general, the research that is the most easily commercialized involves new technology.[33] Research that is successfully commercialized can have a major impact on the world: Rose and Patterson note that synthetic human insulin, recombinant DNA pharmaceuticals, liquid crystal display (LCD), and even Gatorade all came from university research. In addition to its support of the academic mission of knowledge dissemination, research commercialization may provide economic benefits to faculty and the university as a whole and may aid in faculty recruitment and retention.[34]

Only a small percentage of research in universities has commercial potential, and an even smaller percentage of research is actually commercialized. It is fair to say that, like any new business idea, a lot of things have to go right for research to be commercially successful, and it is easy for any of these factors to go wrong.

Businesspeople working with universities should be aware that there are significant conflict of interest issues associated with research in general, and the commercialization of research in particular. It is easy to imagine how a professor creating a start-up but still employed by the university would encounter such issues. Universities maintain conflict of interest offices to manage these issues, which can be complex and contentious.[35]

The commercialization of university research was accelerated by the Patent and Trademark Law Amendments Act of 1980, also known as the Bayh-Dole Act. This act ensured that universities would have title to federally funded inventions, as well as the responsibility to commercialize them. The act led to the creation of many technology transfer offices at research universities, of which there are now several hundred.[36] Technology transfer offices are "designed to commercialize the inventions developed at the university and generate licensing and royalty income ... for the university."[37]

Research is commercialized through one of two major paths, licensing to large companies or licensing to start-ups. In licensing, the university makes an agreement to license the technology resulting from research to an existing company, which incorporates it into its product offerings. In start-ups, university researchers and others form a new enterprise to commercialize products stemming from the research. Technologies that have certain characteristics such as being more incremental, being of moderate value to customers, and having weak intellectual property protection are more likely to be licensed to established companies. Those that are more radical with significant value to customers and strong intellectual property protection are more likely to be the basis for a start-up.[38] The likelihood of start-up formation is also increased by the prestige of the university and by university policies for royalty-sharing that are favorable to faculty entrepreneurs.[39]

Overall commercialization success, whether through licensing or start-ups, is facilitated by a strong set of university policies, an appropriate infrastructure, a university culture supporting commercialization, and a capable technology transfer office. Success can be assessed using metrics such as number of patents, patents per research grant dollar, and royalty income. Private, technology-infused universities like the Massachusetts Institute of Technology and Stanford University perform very well in this space, but public universities like the University of Florida and the University of Utah also have done very well.[40]

Our first example of research in this chapter was faculty working on a better cure for a disease. An example of the commercialization of this kind of research is Spyryx Biosciences, whose formation was based on discoveries of University of North Carolina–Chapel Hill professor Robert Tarran. Dr. Tarran's work has been funded by the NIH and by the North Carolina Biotechnology Center and focuses on the regulation of fluid in the airway. It has potential implications for both cystic fibrosis and chronic obstructive pulmonary disorder; there currently is no cure for either disease. Spyryx was founded in 2013 and received Series A funding of $18 million in 2015 from a set of venture capital firms, including Hatteras Venture Partners.[41] The creation of Spyryx was facilitated by Carolina KickStart, a unit of UNC's technology transfer office, the Office of Commercialization and Economic Development, which helps

UNC researchers commercialize their discoveries. Spyryx currently has several drugs in various stages of clinical trials.[42]

It would be a mistake to think of commercialization as the ultimate indicator of research success. A great deal of research cannot be commercialized, but as created knowledge, it has a significant impact on both local communities and economies and the world.[43] In *The Great American University*, Jonathan Cole identifies a number of such research discoveries—for example, that Vitamin A supplements can reduce malaria and maternal death in the developing world.[44]

8

Where Does College and University Funding Come From? Where Does It Go?

We observed in chapter 1 that as nonprofit organizations, universities are oriented toward mission and reputation rather than financial gain. But understanding their finances is crucially important to understanding academic institutions and how to make them better. In this chapter we provide an overview of the financial aspects of colleges and universities: sources and uses of funds, accounting methods, and budgeting systems. We also discuss administrative bloat—is it real or not? And we end with a discussion of initiatives that academic institutions undertake to enhance their financial positions and more effectively achieve their missions.

What Are the Sources of Funding at Colleges and Universities?

We have already touched on a number of the sources of funding for academic institutions. In chapter 2 we discussed funding in private and public universities, specifically that the former depend more on tuition and the latter more on state funding and that there are downward pressures on both. One implication of downward pressure on tuition is the increasing gap between published tuition (list price) and what the average student actually pays (net tuition, or net price). Colleges offer grants (discounts) to many students to encourage them to enroll, but a large discount rate endangers the college's financial solvency.[1] A recent study by the National Association of College and University Business

Officers estimated that the average discount for first-year students in private institutions in 2018 is up to nearly 50 percent.[2]

Also in chapter 2 we discussed endowments and how they differ among types of universities. A few prominent private institutions have enormous endowments. For most institutions, endowments are a more modest but still important source of funds. In chapter 7 we identified externally funded research as a source of revenue—and at least as big a source of costs—for research universities. We also explained federal and private funding for the indirect costs of research.

In chapter 1 we briefly touched on the aspects of universities that are like businesses, generally known as auxiliaries, including residence halls, dining halls, and bookstores. These operations are at a minimum expected to break even, so as not to drain funding away from the academic enterprise. They generally earn at least a small operating margin, which can be used for maintenance, special projects, capital improvements, and the like. In some cases, operations like the bookstore will have a significant enough margin to contribute meaningfully to the academic mission of the institution. At UNC–Chapel Hill, for example, this margin is used to fund student scholarships (see chapter 9).

Philanthropy is, of course, an important source of funding for academic institutions. Many readers have likely been involved in fundraising for universities, making or asking for gifts. Institutions may set a threshold for what they consider major gifts—for example, $100,000 or more. We discussed earlier how endowments work, as a relatively consistent source of funds. Major gifts to universities may go to an endowment, in which case they will provide a flow of funds to the institution indefinitely. Or they may be expendable, so that their impact is initially more significant but is not sustained. Further, gifts may be given at the institution level or at the school or department level.

Most major gifts are given for a specific purpose, and the use of these funds is restricted to this purpose. They may fund a distinguished chair for a faculty member or a scholarship program for students. They may fund a new building or an athletic facility. Unrestricted gifts, which can be used at the discretion of the president or dean, are rare and valuable. The biggest gifts, like the biggest endowments, are mostly given to a small number of prestigious, mostly private, institutions.[3]

Gifts whose value is below the major gift threshold are considered annual fund gifts. These smaller gifts, which may be only twenty-five or fifty dollars for young alumni or well into the thousands, add up to a substantial amount of funding, the use of which is at the discretion of the dean or president. These gifts are solicited through periodic outreach to alumni. University fund-raisers stress that consistent giving of small amounts as a young alum is an important predictor of major gifts later in one's life.

One element of philanthropy that is implicit in our discussion is that many gifts involve the institution doing something new that consumes the gift: erecting a building, hiring a professor, or creating a new academic program. This activity certainly helps the institution, but ironically it can lead to constructing new buildings while current buildings deteriorate or to hiring expensive new professors while current professors are underpaid. This is why unrestricted gifts are so important, as they can be used according to institutional priorities, including support for current employees and strategic initiatives.

At UNC–Chapel Hill, 22 percent of revenues in 2017 came from state appropriations, 40 percent from research grants, 15 percent from private gifts, and 24 percent from tuition and fees. We recently reviewed financial data from several prominent public research universities.[4] The percentage of their total budget coming from state support ranged from 11 to 22 percent. The research component ranged from 22 to 40 percent. The funding coming from gifts and grants ranged from 12 to 22 percent. And finally, the amount represented by tuition and fees ranged from 24 to 45 percent. So even institutions that are similar in mission and scope can have significant differences in funding models.[5]

By comparison, Carnegie Mellon University, which as a private institution receives no state support, reports that roughly 37 percent of its revenue comes from research, 15 percent from gifts, and 49 percent from tuition and fees.[6] For smaller private universities like Gonzaga, the vast majority of funding (80 to 90 percent) comes from tuition and fees.[7] Finally, Pomona College receives about 2 percent of its revenues from funded research, 35 percent from gifts, and 63 percent from tuition and fees.[8] As Goldie Blumenstyk explains, "Except for a lucky few dozen of the wealthiest colleges, tuition is the major source of revenue for all colleges."[9]

How Are Funds Allocated?

Colleges and universities use a variety of budget models to allocate funds.[10] The budgeting model determines how the university decides how much money is allocated to each unit, with the objective being a distribution that best supports the mission. We will focus here on a few of the most common models. For this section to make sense, remember from chapter 2 that universities are made up of smaller units, such as a liberal arts college and a set of professional schools. Baccalaureate colleges must determine how funds are allocated to academic departments, which is somewhat simpler. In all cases, the budget model also has to decide how the nonacademic units on campus will be funded.

In the incremental budget model, which is the most commonly used model in higher education, base funding for units stays the same from year to year, and only new money is allocated across the schools.[11] Allocations are made centrally, after each school has the opportunity to make its budget case. This means that an institution-wide perspective can be brought to budget decisions. Of course, what comes up must go down, and central administration also has to make cuts when resources decline.

An alternative model is the Responsibility Center Management (RCM) model. Unlike the incremental model, the allocation methods are transparent and do not involve annual decisions by senior leaders. At the heart of this model is the agreement to allocate budget dollars using a set of formulas, which essentially replaces senior leader decisions. Most institutions that use RCM review the allocation formulas on a regular basis and make changes to reflect new priorities or to address unintended consequences of the model.[12] This model is used most often in private research universities but is increasingly being used in large public universities.

An extreme version of the RCM model is ETOB, which stands for "every tub on its own bottom."[13] While most budget models involve cross-subsidization among schools (also known as subvention), in the ETOB model, each school keeps the money that it raises from tuition, gifts, research, and so on and pays its own costs. Schools do not receive funds from central administration, nor do they subsidize one another. In this system, each school is taxed to pay for central services, such as the library. Obviously this is a radically decentralized model, in which schools need to ensure that they are consistently financially viable. The advantages of this model include its simplicity and transparency and its incentives for entrepreneurial behavior among schools. Its main disadvantage is budget unpredictability for schools. The ETOB budget model and to a lesser extent all RCM models can be considered market-based systems, while the incremental budget model is more of a central planning system.

Vanderbilt University uses this ETOB type of budget model, which they call VU-ETOB. As Vanderbilt provost Susan Wente describes it, "Under the ... VU-ETOB budget model, all revenues flow directly to the school or college from which it was generated and each school and college is therefore responsible for directly paying their own expenses."[14] This model is relatively new for Vanderbilt and replaces a more centralized model.

Capital budgeting is also an important process for colleges and universities, which have large and, in many cases, old physical plants. In private universities, decisions about capital projects are made by the senior leadership and the board. In public universities, the state legislature or the system governing board may also be involved in these decisions. We noted earlier that many universities have significant levels of deferred maintenance. Donors are more likely to fund a new building, which may be named for them, than support the repair of an existing building, which is likely already named for someone else.[15]

It is important for board members to understand university budgeting, especially its potential to offset deficits from lower student enrollment or declining state support (for public institutions). There is a common misunderstanding particularly around why university endowment and research funding cannot be used to offset declining state support. Universities are restricted, by law and agreement with donors, from using the corpus of the endowment.[16] Further, research funding is not fungible; that is, funding for research cannot be used to offset other costs.

Where Are Funds Spent?

As in other professional service organizations, the biggest category of spending in colleges and universities is on people. In higher education organizations, the biggest chunk of funding goes toward the people who provide instruction, between one-third and one-half in every Carnegie Classification, according to EAB research.[17] Academic support and student services are also major cost categories at all types of institutions, whereas research is a major factor only in public and private research institutions (like Carnegie Mellon and UNC–Chapel Hill).

What Is Administrative Bloat, and Is It Real?

The claim of administrative bloat is that colleges and universities have significantly higher costs due to expanded amenities and increasing numbers of unnecessary, highly paid administrators, which have led to considerably higher tuition.[18] We have already mentioned in chapter 2 that tuition indeed has gone up and that for public universities part of the reason is the reduction in public support for higher education on a per-student basis. Paul Campos, in an influential 2015 *New York Times* article, calculated that tuition at public universities has nearly quadrupled over the last thirty-five years.[19] While Campos states that total support for public institutions is higher than in the past, he acknowledges that support actually is lower on a per-student basis and that there are many more students now than there were a few decades ago. But he cites Department of Education data that show that "administrative positions at colleges and universities grew by 60 percent between 1993 and 2009, which Bloomberg reported was 10 times the rate of growth of tenured faculty positions." He claims, without using any data, that the compensation for these administrators is excessive and dismisses out of hand arguments that higher administrative salaries are driven by market factors.

How compelling is his argument? Are administrative costs the primary driver of higher tuition? And are these administrators superfluous? Other writers, including significantly Matt Reed, have questioned Campos's analysis. An early sentence in Reed's rejoinder to the *NYT* article gives one a sense of this debate: "As with so much of your coverage of higher education, the column is both a failure and a mess, and the two are related."[20]

Benjamin Landy also disagrees with Campos and attributes rising costs to drastically reduced public funding for higher education: "Per-student revenue from state and local governments fell by $2,600, after adjusting for inflation, between 1987 and 2012. During that same period, per-student tuition increased by $2,600. In other words, the entire increase in tuition at public colleges and universities over the last 25 years has gone to make up for declining state and local revenue, leaving no additional funding available to improve programs and services or fund costs that are rising faster than the rate of inflation, such as employee health care."[21] Similarly, and in direct response to Campos's claim that vanishing state funding is a "fairy tale," Robert Hiltonsmith writes,

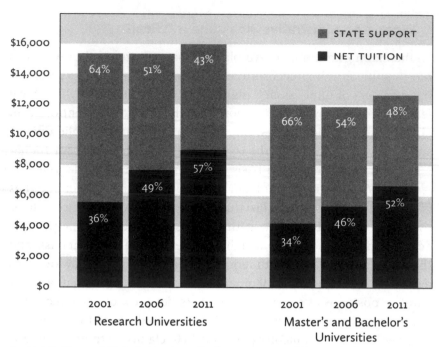

8.1. Net Tuition and State Support per Student, 2001–2011 (Shares of Education and Related Spending). *Source: Policyshop.*

Huh? This is so badly wrong that I wonder how it possibly got by the *Times'* fact-checkers. Campos claims that aggregate state higher education funding is in fact skyrocketing, citing its rise from $11.1 billion in 1960 to $86.6 billion in 2009. Neglecting the reality that state funding has since declined to $78.8 billion as of 2013, the huge flaw with [Campos's] claim is that it ignores the equally rapid rise in enrollment at public universities, whose population has grown nearly 500 percent, from 2.5 million students in 1961 to nearly 15 million in 2013. Campos ignores this huge increase, despite the fact that nearly every reputable expert on higher education reports funding in per-student terms, and for good reason: because ignoring it would be irresponsible.[22]

To illustrate his point, Hiltonsmith provides a graph (see graph 8.1) that shows net tuition and state support per student from 2001 to 2011.

Apart from decreased state funding for public higher education, increased costs on college campuses derive from a number of sources, which calls into question the argument that bloated and unnecessary administration is the main or only driver. One cost is compliance with federal government regulations, which we touched on in chapter 4. Compliance with regulations that concern all organizations (such as EPA regulations) as well as with those that affect primarily colleges and universities (such as Title IX and the Clery Act) is expensive. And these costs largely are reflected in a greater number of administrators.

Increasingly sophisticated information technology systems also have led to higher costs in higher education. This point may seem counter-intuitive, but most colleges and universities maintain, for example, a significant staff simply to protect their networks from attacks. The provision of Wi-Fi to every square inch on campus and the use of systems to provide real-time information to students and faculty also add to technology infrastructure costs.

Some increased administrative costs are for items that most people would see as entirely legitimate, or at least unavoidable.[23] For example, expectations for student services have dramatically increased. Many universities are spending much more on career counseling, as well as on mental health counseling; students and parents understandably expect these services. As the people providing these services generally are not professors, they would be considered administrators, thus contributing to "bloat"—which then raises the question of whether this "bloat" is necessarily a bad thing.[24] Faculty member and author Robert Kelchen thinks not: "Faculty do complain about all of the assistant and associate deans out there, but this workload would otherwise fall on faculty. And given the research, teaching, and service expectations that we face, we can't take on those roles."[25]

A related point is that universities have dramatically altered their philosophies on student success, leading to higher costs. The famous dean's orientation talk that stated, "Look to your left, look to your right, only one of you will succeed here" would be unthinkable today. Universities closely track retention and graduation rates; they want all of their students to succeed, and they provide academic support using sophisticated and expensive IT tools and academic counseling to promote this goal. Institutions strive to provide exemplary services and infrastructure in support of their students and also in their broader efforts to stay ahead in an increasingly competitive market.

Finally, the facilities provided by colleges and universities are much nicer than a generation ago. Every parent we know who has taken a campus tour has been blown away by the residence halls, the dining facilities, and the recreation opportunities, among other amenities. Only some of these costs would be reflected in greater numbers of administrators.

Administrative bloat is not the principal driver of rising costs in higher education. An August 2018 report from the Midwestern Higher Education Compact summarizes this argument and explains three macroeconomic factors attributed to rising costs in higher education:

> Rising college cost is driven substantially by three economy-wide forces: (1) Lagging productivity growth is endemic to personal service industries, so service prices rise faster than goods prices. This is called "cost disease"; (2) The higher education workforce is highly educated and the cost of hiring highly educated workers has risen sharply since 1981; and (3) A college's mission and market require it to meet a rising standard of educational care. More than any [malady or] potential dysfunction on campus, these three factors have led to rising real costs.
>
> Administrative "bloat" and amenity competitions [such as "luxury" residence halls or improved student services] grab headlines but do not account for much of the rising cost. Rising numbers of professional staff and improved amenities are not inherently inefficient.[26]

How Is Financial Reporting Done in Academic Institutions?

While Generally Accepted Accounting Principles apply to all higher education institutions, private and public institutions rely on different accounting standards. Private institutions rely on accounting standards issued by the Financial Accounting Standards Board, and public institutions rely on those standards issued by the Governmental Accounting Standards Board. A report from Hanover Research states, "The financial reporting for FASB entities is intended to educate investors and creditors on the financial status of private universities, while the GASB documents are used to support transparency of public and taxpayer money provided by government funding."[27] Differences between standards — for example in balance sheet and cash flow reporting — make it difficult to compare financial statements from different types of institutions.

One important difference between university and business accounting is that many universities use fund accounting. The administrative guide for Stanford University explains, "Because the University receives funding from a variety of sources, with different types of terms and restrictions, each source must be tracked as a separate accounting entity in a unique fund."[28] This means that deficits in one fund or fund group cannot be offset by surpluses in another.

What Do Universities Do to Enhance Their Financial Positions?

Faced with all of the challenges we have described in previous chapters, colleges and universities have undertaken many different initiatives to strengthen their finances. We have already discussed several of them, all of which to some degree could be controversial:

- Raising tuition. This was for many years a simple and largely effective strategy from the point of view of the institutions but not for students and their families, and it is rarely sustainable.
- Selectively discounting stated tuition by providing grants based on families' strength and ability to pay. Universities use discounting in order to attract and recruit students in a time of declining enrollments, even though it can strain their tuition and fee revenue.[29]
- Accepting, at public universities, an increasing number of nonresident (out-of-state and international) students who pay higher tuition.
- Hiring more faculty who are not on the tenure track. These faculty are paid less and may be terminated when cost-cutting is necessary. One university recently advertised for alumni to serve as volunteer (unpaid) adjunct faculty, which must be the reductio ad absurdum for this strategy.[30]
- Implementing online courses and programs to address a different market from the traditional residential student market.
- Cutting costs through budget reductions. These reductions often affect operations and programs.

Academic institutions are using a number of other strategies to enhance their finances, including the following:

- Using data analysis to optimize course and section offerings, such as combining three lower-enrollment sections into two with higher enrollment.[31]

- Introducing shared services organizations to cut costs. For example, human resources, IT, or finance staff may be consolidated across departments and schools to provide services more efficiently.[32] Academic institutions have had a wide range of outcomes when implementing shared services, and this approach has been enormously controversial at several colleges.[33] In some ways this resembles the centralization of the procurement function that is now commonplace in universities, except that the benefits of centralized procurement have more to do with the pricing power of scale and negotiating lower prices than with reducing the number of people who do procurement.
- Using business mindsets and techniques to reduce costs while preserving service quality. For example, the University of New Hampshire recently has implemented lean management approaches to reduce costs in both academic and nonacademic areas.[34] More than 700 employees have been involved in working on over 100 processes.
- Selling or leasing assets to private organizations, which in many cases can operate these assets (such as power plants) more efficiently and despite needing to make a profit can improve the financial return on these assets for the institution. The biggest example of this kind of arrangement is Ohio State's $483 million fifty-year deal with CampusParc.[35] Of course, this kind of deal is not new in principle, only in scale. Universities have been partnering with private organizations for years to run dining halls and campus bookstores.[36]

Costs at colleges and universities are increasing for a variety of reasons. Some costs involve facilities intended to attract students. Many involve people who do not teach, such as administrators, but many of these individuals are doing work that is either required (government compliance) or expected (student mental health or career counseling). So, it is a stretch to sustain the argument that rising costs are singularly a function of unnecessary layers of administration. It is worth pointing out that this claim is consistent with the faculty-centric point of view described in chapter 6—that any activity not performed by faculty is suspect and should be minimized. Many universities are using innovative approaches to cut costs and improve revenue streams.

Recommendations for Business and University Collaboration

Businesspeople serving on university boards and scholars leading those universities are highly intelligent, accomplished, thoughtful, motivated, and hard-working people. If both sides would assume that they have much to learn from the other—that the experience of businesspeople can help the university solve its problems and that the academic approach for research, teaching, and service has evolved because it works reasonably well—then the rhetoric would lessen, and the two sides could work together for good.
—Doug Shackelford

We created this book to become the indispensable source of understanding colleges and universities for businesspeople who need to know about them and want to help them. We hope that we have provided thorough answers and rich context to the questions that businesspeople and board members have asked us. Many who come from outside higher education play a critical role in the success of colleges and universities. University board members and others engaged in important enterprises within universities, such as prospective donors, vendors, legislators, consultants, and senior administrative leaders, make critical decisions about strategic institutional priorities, senior-level hiring, and institutional funding. With a deeper and more measured understanding of higher education, they are better equipped to affect the success of the institutions they serve. Their contributions are critical. Increasingly, in an environment of shrinking resources and intense competition, leaders in higher education must be able to make a sound and sustainable business case for their institutions.

A friend in state government dismissively commented to one of us, "I don't speak academic." This remark was meant in jest, but it was cause for concern. Colleges and universities occupy a central place in American society and have tremendous economic impact, and yet often these institutions are misunderstood and unfairly maligned by the very people whose support and influence are most needed. Justin

Stover in the *Chronicle of Higher Education* observes, "The contemporary university is a strange chimera. It has become an institution for teaching undergraduates, a lab for medical and technological development in partnership with industry, a hospital, a museum (or several), a performance hall, a radio station, a landowner, a big-money (or money-losing) sports club, a research center competing for government funding—often the biggest employer for a hundred miles around—and, for a few institutions, a hedge fund ('with a small college attached for tax purposes,' adds one wag)."[1] And of course in addition, colleges and universities are key sources of employees for local, national, and international firms.

In writing this book we hope we have provided a more complete and comprehensive illustration of American colleges and universities, which are essential to creating an educated citizenry, developing our creativity and ingenuity, advancing our ability to solve problems both large and small, promoting our entrepreneurship and economy, and fostering our social mobility, well-being, and empathy for others. Our wish is that this book will have a lasting impact on businesspeople's engagement with colleges and universities. Moreover, we hope that by better understanding these institutions, businesspeople (and anyone not from an academic background who works with universities) will engage with them and invest in their success. But the record of businesspeople helping academic institutions is mixed, as the examples in the introduction demonstrate. As we discussed, businesspeople can become frustrated because, since they do not fully understand the nature of academic organizations, their ideas and suggestions are not always feasible and not always welcome.

A frequent question raised in the interaction between businesspeople and higher education concerns whether colleges and universities should be run more like businesses. While colleges and universities are not businesses, they have businesslike problems, including management of revenues and costs, the need to be strategic, the need to manage people, and the need to market the institution. And indeed, it is an inescapable fact that academic institutions are run much more like businesses than they were just a few decades ago. As former college president Richard Freeland wrote, "Colleges have gotten better at thinking systematically about how to flourish in the intensely competitive academic marketplace, and with this has come, in many cases, more thoughtful approaches to setting priorities, more rational and efficient uses of resources, more effective approaches to recruiting students and awarding financial aid, and more sophisticated administration of non-academic functions. Taken as a whole, these changes have enabled institutions to do a better job of serving students and fulfilling their missions."[2]

Many businesspeople would like to take this process of applying business principles to institutions of higher education even further. On the other hand, many academics think it has gone too far already. Tim McGinley, a longtime board member at Purdue University, told us, "Higher ed is a unique entity, with a unique culture and way of doing things. The biggest mistake is to assume it should be imitating business all the time. There are business principles, but you have to understand what higher education is all about and what the institution is all about."[3] We think this statement suggests the desired approach to applying business ideas in academic settings. Richard Freeland makes a similar point in saying that we need to remember that higher education is a calling, not just a business enterprise.[4]

The challenges that arise when business leaders and university leaders work together are constant and ongoing. At the time of this writing, the incoming chair of the University of North Carolina System Board of Governors has touted his business background and hopes to bring a more businesslike approach to the leadership of the university system. A recent article outlined both the promise and the potential problems associated with this initiative.[5] UNC Board of Governors chair Harry Smith said his "goal is to run campuses efficiently—control costs and enhance income without making them businesses." In comparison with the confidence expressed in this statement, consider the reflection of David Miles, a university trustee with more than twenty years' experience: "Looking back, I realize just how little I knew—or at least understood—and how long it took me to become a truly effective trustee."[6]

The Imperative for Collaboration between Business and Higher Education

Armed with the information found in this book, businesspeople can influence the success of the colleges and universities that they serve. But in order to do so, business professionals and academic leaders need to collaborate effectively. While collaboration has the familiar meaning of working well together, for our purposes it has a more technical meaning, which comes from research on managing conflict.[7] From this perspective, approaches to conflict management can be characterized by an individual's assertiveness (attempting to satisfy one's own concerns) or cooperativeness (attempting to satisfy another person's concerns).[8] Collaboration is an approach to managing conflict that uniquely combines assertiveness and cooperativeness in an attempt for both parties to satisfy their needs. Many businesspeople understand and express this general idea of collaboration as "win-win."[9]

In collaboration, individuals bring their needs, goals, and skills together to produce outcomes that will benefit everyone. Collaboration requires, of course, that people understand and appreciate one another's perspectives. David Perlmutter describes the tendency for faculty members to be suspicious of board members, and especially deans and presidents, who are not from the academy.[10] One of our faculty colleagues commented, "Too many academics speak of businesspeople as though they are dullards whose usefulness ends with their philanthropy. There's an unstated assumption that, if they were all that brilliant, they would have a PhD."[11]

For effective collaboration, faculty members must change their attitudes about businesspeople, just as businesspeople must leave behind suspicions about academics (and we hope that this book helps them in this process). Effective collaboration happens within healthy organizations. Former university president Susan Resnick Pierce explains, "At dysfunctional institutions, trustees often view the faculty as unproductive obstructionists. In contrast, in healthy institutions trustees view the faculty with respect and appreciation."[12]

Here are some ways to understand why and how collaboration is critical to colleges and universities.

Differentiation and Integration

A number of years ago, two prominent Harvard Business School professors explored the issue of how people representing different business functions (for example, research and sales) should work together.[13] Paul Lawrence and Jay Lorsch used two key concepts, differentiation ("the segmentation of the organization into subsystems, each of which tends to develop particular attributes") and integration ("the process of achieving unity of effort among the various subsystems in the accomplishment of the organization's task"). Interestingly, time orientation was among the elements of differentiation. Their research asked, "What patterns of differentiation and integration are associated with organizational success?"[14]

Based on a study of six organizations in the chemicals industry, the authors concluded that (as one would expect) pairs of organizational functions that were more differentiated had more difficulty achieving integration. Given the many differences between businesspeople and academics, this finding is consistent with the idea that achieving unity of effort in their work together in higher education would be, well, challenging. But the really interesting finding of the study was that the best-performing organizations had high levels of both differentiation *and* integration. In other words, in higher performing organizations, people in segmented functions maintained their differences but found ways to integrate their perspectives. Integration was characterized by having, for example, cross-functional teams and by embracing a style of conflict management that confronted (not avoided) problems and solved them collectively.

The implication of this research for businesspeople in universities is that the differences in perspective between businesspeople and academics are valuable and should not be minimized or avoided. Board members should maintain their ways of thinking rather than surrender to what they understand to be the norms of higher education. And academics should retain their perspectives rather than abandon them to minimize conflict in their work with businesspeople. In Lawrence and Lorsch's study, among organizations with similar levels of integration, those with greater differentiation among functions were more effective. The most effective organizations maintained differences in perspective but found ways to work in an integrative way to seek common goals. While the setting for their research was different, these findings strike us as something to aspire to in higher education.

Diversity and Inclusion

Another imperative for effective collaboration between businesspeople and academics comes from contemporary approaches to diversity and inclusion in business. While some discussion of diversity and inclusion may have political overtones, the core insight of this perspective is that group and organizational performance is enhanced by diversity of thinking, especially among leaders and managers. Differences in race, ethnicity, gender identity, sexual orientation, and so on are seen as proxies for differences in how people think about situations and approach solutions. Of course, diversity is effective only when it is paired with inclusion—that is, when all individuals have the opportunity to participate and engage actively in organizational decision-making and problem-solving.

A number of studies support the relationship between diversity and inclusion with organizational performance. Recent research by McKinsey & Company found that companies with the greatest gender, racial, and ethnic diversity generally outperformed the typical company in their industry, while the least diverse companies were less productive and less successful.[15] A recent study by Rocio Lorenzo and Martin Reeves yielded similar conclusions.[16] In a study of 1,700 companies in eight countries, they found that diversity among managers was associated with greater organizational innovation and profitability.

The work of Margaret Neale and her colleagues at the Stanford Graduate School of Business provides more nuanced conclusions about the relationship between diversity and organizational performance. Reflecting on several specific studies, Neale concludes, "What you don't see is diversity having a direct performance effect.... The kind of conflict that exists and how the team handles the conflict will determine whether this diversity is effective in increasing ... performance."[17]

Of course, as we have discussed, businesspeople and academics have vastly different training and experience and different ways of approaching problems. These differences may well cause conflict, which may or may not lead to better organizational performance. It seems likely that effective collaboration can result in creative new solutions to the myriad challenges facing academic institutions. Of course, if businesspeople and academics do not work together collaboratively and effectively, these benefits are lost.

Recommendations for Businesspeople Serving as Trustees and Senior Academic Leaders

Whether we think about these issues in terms of differentiation and integration or diversity and inclusion, organizational performance is improved by people with different perspectives coming together to solve problems collectively. Here we present specific recommendations for how this can be accomplished in the college and university setting.

Ensure that there is effective onboarding and ongoing development for new board members and leaders coming from business. As we have demonstrated in this book, there is much to learn. Mistakes based on ignorance can be costly. A wealth of knowledge from the field of talent management can be helpful in designing effective onboarding experiences. A few hours or a couple of days at the beginning of someone's tenure may work as orientation but will not remotely suffice as onboarding, which should take place over a period of months. Michael Watkins's book *The First 90 Days* may be helpful for onboarding trustees and academic leaders.[18]

Find a way to leverage those individuals who can connect the business and academic communities, sometimes known as "boundary spanners." These may be businesspeople with prior experience in higher education, or academics who have some business experience, perhaps in start-ups or as consultants. One academic leader with a business background we interviewed said that the most valuable people for moving universities forward are "of the tribe but on the bus," meaning faculty with credibility in the academic community who perceive the need for change. Of course, one of the goals of this book is to help businesspeople learn how to span the boundary with academics.

Businesspeople should choose their words carefully, especially when they are new, so as not to lose their credibility, harm their reputation, or burn bridges. Examples of what not to do: one university board member called for a "public hanging," while another volunteered that "tenure is stupid." It is perhaps unfair that unguarded comments such as these could spell the end of the road for a board member, dean, or president, but that is the world we are living in. Sometimes in the academy what one says may be more noteworthy than what one does.[19]

Board members and leaders of public colleges and universities should become familiar with the public record and meeting laws (also known as "sunshine laws") in their state and act accordingly. In many states, laws allow journalists or citizens to request emails and text messages and the like created in the course of the work of the institution, and the institution must provide them. Comments made in what was intended to be a private exchange can be excruciating to read in the newspaper.

Make every effort to arrange for board members to meet and talk with students and faculty and to learn about their courses, research, and service projects. (These meetings happen much more naturally with presidents and deans.) We have often seen board members become fascinated with a course, a research project, or the life story of a student based on such conversations and interactions. In the absence of real connections on campus, it is too easy for businesspeople to buy into anecdotes or labels (such as "ivory tower," summers off, "snowflakes," and so on). It is interesting that these dynamics extend even to professional schools, as indicated in this story told by an accounting professor who does research on taxes:

> A mutual friend invited me to lunch with a tax attorney who serves on the [university board]. The attorney asked me with a touch of skepticism, "What exactly does a tax researcher do?" Given the attorney's expertise, I could get technical with him about my own work. Within a minute, he conceded, "That's important stuff." When I added that I had testified before Congress on multiple occasions and that congressional staffers read my research, he was sold that my research matters. But soon he reverted to his prior idea that business schools should be about "practical" things, not theoretical academic work, asking (again with some edge), "OK, I can see that tax research is important, but what about 'accounting' research? What could you possibly research about accounting?" A few examples from our faculty and he was won over again. And by the end of the lunch, he was completely sold on the business school. This is not a unique experience for me.[20]

Faculty members—especially those with tenure—might do and say things that businesspeople find outrageous and that would be treated as fireable insubordination in most businesses. One faculty member we know was described by a university leader as "a bull who carries his own china shop around with him."[21] As difficult as it may be, businesspeople should try not to let them get under their skin. Focusing on finding clever ways to punish them is a distraction from the real job of helping to move the institution forward and frankly is beneath the dignity of trustees and presidents. We have seen a board devote enormous resources to just such retribution, cutting budgets and closing units. It was an unfortunate, embarrassing, and ultimately meaningless display of power.

Board members and senior administrators have every right to expect that those who report to them can articulate the direction in which they want to lead their university or unit, the steps they are taking to get there, and the measures of their success. Academic goals are inherently different from business goals (see chapter 1), but they are not (or at least should not be) nonexistent. We also urge skepticism toward Byzantine plans with layers of priorities and scores of implementation steps. This approach unfortunately is fairly common in higher education and should be discouraged. Focus is no less important in academics than in business, perhaps even more important, given the limited resources at most institutions. Trustees should expect academic leaders to provide a clear and sustainable business case for their institution. This would include strategy and metrics as well as the financial scenarios, plans, and assumptions that underpin the aspirations of the academic leaders. If the board and the senior leaders can agree on this, they will have a solid basis on which to work together.[22]

Along similar lines, trustees of public colleges and universities in particular need to fulfill their responsibility for ensuring financial discipline. While truly wasteful spending is probably less rampant than anecdotes about rock-climbing walls would lead us to believe (and wasteful is, to some extent, in the eye of the beholder), it does happen. In order to exercise financial discipline, trustees and presidents must understand how investments will advance important institutional goals (how much improvement? in what time period? with what level of certainty?) and what other opportunities are being forgone to make the investment. In both public and private universities, maintaining reasonable and competitive tuition levels should be part of this conversation.[23]

Board members can often have a real impact on the business components of the college or university. When a board member's expertise matches an institutional need, it can lead to great results. In the best case, cost savings or revenue enhancements from business activities can be used to support the academic mission. It is important, however, that such involvement be undertaken with the knowledge and consent of the president. Board members' circumventing the president to work directly with university business officers undermines the president's authority and credibility, and this represents poor governance.

In working with academic institutions, businesspeople should present business principles in ways that are consistent with academic values. For example, people in the academy care deeply about the creation and dissemination of knowledge. As long as business principles are consistent with these bedrock values, academics should be open to the new approaches they represent. But if business leaders are not sensitive to these core academic values, the academy will tend to reject business suggestions, even if the suggestions are seemingly harmless.[24] For example, improving purchasing policies could be framed simply as a good business practice that eliminates waste or instead packaged as a way to save money that can be redirected toward student scholarships.

Liz DiMarco Weinmann urges academic leaders to "accept the fact that you may have to adjust your leadership style from what was effective in other situations."[25] We have identified a great number of differences between the commercial and academic worlds, so it makes sense that a different approach to leadership would be called for in transitioning from one to the other. Certainly, recognizing the differences in goals, governance, and hierarchy will require some leadership adjustment from most executives.

To expand the previous point, David Perlmutter asks college presidents to remember that "you are not 'the boss.' You are a coalition builder."[26] This makes perfect sense in light of our discussion in chapter 6 of organization and influence in academic institutions. A business leader who expects businesslike deference in an academic setting will be disappointed. People in the academy need to be convinced of the value of plans and are unlikely to accept anything based simply on authority. Perlmutter concludes his article on academic leadership by nonacademics as follows: "While someone who is experienced in our profession might have an advantage, an outsider *can* succeed—but only if she or he takes seriously the task of understanding the culture of academe, the political constituencies of the campus, and our often subtle and nuanced methods of persuasion and coalition building."

A final point for business leaders about working with faculty: you will find that you will not be able to establish common ground with everyone, despite sincere efforts. Some academics do not see the benefits of applying business thinking to academic problems, just as some businesspeople cannot appreciate the contributions of the academic way of thinking. This is okay. You won't need everyone's buy-in to make substantive change (and you probably don't get this in a business setting, either).

The UNC–Chapel Hill Student Stores Initiative

We end both this chapter and the book with a case study of the decision to outsource the Josephus Daniels Student Stores (simply known as Student Stores),[27] the independent campus bookstore at UNC–Chapel Hill, to Barnes & Noble College. This case is meant to elaborate on a number of points we have made in the book. It provides a helpful example of collaboration among interested parties when a university faces an important business decision.[28]

Student Stores has been part of UNC–Chapel Hill for 100 years. The current facility was built in the 1960s and is located in the middle of campus, adjacent to the Pit—the area in front of the bookstore that serves as a sort of town center/village green for the university and arguably is the center of campus life.[29] Student Stores has provided textbooks, school supplies, spirit wear, computers, and many other items to the campus community. It has also long been the home of the Bull's Head Bookshop, a small bookstore-within-a-store located next to the coffee bar. Faculty and students enjoy browsing through Bull's Head and cherish its role in the intellectual life of the university. Bull's Head has had a particular focus on books by Carolina faculty and other local authors. Unfortunately, it had been losing money for some time. However, as English professor Beverly Taylor said, perhaps representing the view of many faculty members, "There was something about the smallness that made it feel very homey, not corporate."

Prior to 2016, the university itself had always operated Student Stores, and profits from the store as a whole—roughly $400,000 annually on sales of about $25 million—were used by law to fund undergraduate student scholarships. Due to the financial pressures we have discussed in previous chapters, UNC (like many universities) had found it increasingly difficult to fund undergraduate scholarships,

UNC received in 2015 an unsolicited proposal from Follett, a very large campus retailer in higher education, to take over the operation of Student Stores. Follett's proposal suggested that the organization could improve revenues so that profits would increase to $3 million annually. The claim was premised on Follett's purchasing power, which would lower acquisition costs of books and other materials, as well as on the introduction of efficiencies based on its national operation of over 1,000 bookstores. Follett also offered the ability of a large chain operator of bookstores to sell textbooks returned at the end of a semester. Vice Chancellor for Finance and Administration Matt Fajack was quoted at the time as saying, "[If] we get an offer for that much money … we have a duty to take a look at it."[30] Similarly, the university's board of trustees encouraged UNC to take the proposal seriously.

This would not be UNC's first partnership with an outside organization to operate a campus facility. The Carolina Inn, the university's iconic hotel, as well as the Rizzo Conference Center have been operated by outside organizations (currently Destination Hotels) for some time. And Carolina Dining Services has partnered with Aramark for nearly twenty years.

Yet the idea to outsource Student Stores was greeted with opposition from some faculty and students and, not surprisingly, the store's employees and management. In September 2015 about 200 students gathered in the Pit to protest, and more than 3,500 people signed a change.org petition against the proposal. The Employee Forum, which represents university staff, also came out against the privatization of Student Stores.[31] The main concerns of those opposing were the fate of the forty-nine Student Stores employees and the potential closing or repurposing of Bull's Head. Underlying, however, was certainly some opposition in principle to more corporate involvement in university operations. As Professor Taylor put it, "Many faculty are anxious about the corporatization of higher ed and attention to STEM versus the humanities and fine arts."

In response to the Follett proposal and in the context of the opposition mounted against the idea of privatization, the university decided to solicit multiple bids for the operation of the bookstore and form a committee to review the bids and make a recommendation. The committee was chaired by Associate Vice Chancellor for Campus Enterprises Brad Ives. Ives is an alumnus who attended the university as a Morehead Scholar and attained both a UNC bachelor's degree and a law degree. Prior to returning to work at UNC, he was employed in structured finance, investment management, and solar panel manufacturing and as assistant secretary for natural resources for the state of North Carolina. Ives describes his time on the committee as challenging, as his fellow alums would approach him at receptions and ask him, "How could you do this?"[32]

The committee included two representatives of student government, two representatives of the Employee Forum, two faculty representatives, and staff from Auxiliary Services (the campus unit that was cur-

9.1. Student Stores protests in the Pit at the University of North Carolina at Chapel Hill in April 2016, when the university decided to outsource its bookstore to Barnes & Noble College. (Chris Seward, *News and Observer*)

rently responsible for the store) and the provost's office. Professors Lloyd Kramer (history) and Beverly Taylor (English and comparative literature) were approached by faculty chair Dr. Bruce Cairns to join the committee. They both were initially negative about the privatization initiative, and even about being part of the decision process, but they both eventually relented and agreed to serve on the committee. Taylor said, "I was reluctant to serve on the committee. I had a substantial attachment to Student Stores and was hostile to the idea of a business taking it over." Along similar lines, Kramer described himself as "highly skeptical of the proposal." He said, "Student Stores was important in campus life, and the bookstore element was to be downsized. I thought it was the wrong message to send out." As the committee began its deliberations, he added, "My concern was how Student Stores could represent the core intellectual values of the university, especially if Bull's Head disappeared."[33]

The committee established four objectives for the potential Student Stores transition: Student Stores should generate more money for student scholarships; secure three years of guaranteed employment for the employees; keep Bull's Head open and make it better; and make textbooks available at the best possible price, so that the deal was not made to work by charging higher prices to students.

The university published a formal request for proposals and received them from Follett, Barnes & Noble College, and the current management team from Student Stores, as well as more limited proposals (textbooks only) from Amazon and Missouri Book Services. Each organization was also invited to make an in-person presentation to the committee. UNC hired a consultant with expertise in college bookstore management to help the committee in its deliberations. Finally, the committee studied a variety of other bookstores, including those at Harvard, Yale, Boston College, and Boston University. The faculty were impressed by the Harvard Coop, which is run by Barnes & Noble. Ives describes this as "an aha moment."

During this process, the views of Professors Kramer and Taylor began to evolve. As Kramer tells it, "I realized that Student Stores' mode of operating was not well situated for students, and that Bull's Head was collapsing.... The system had more drawbacks than I realized. The only way Student Stores could sustain viability was to close Bull's Head entirely. I thought it would be privatized and our values would be compromised. But I realized the best chance to keep Bull's Head was to go with a private supplier like Barnes & Noble. They would [be able to] maintain the inventory.... So I changed my view. The best way to ensure the strength of our intellectual values was to have a different kind of resource." He added, "Some of my colleagues were baffled.... They were stunned."

Professor Taylor also began to think about the situation differently: "The more I learned about the facts the more I thought that someone with more experience would do a better job." Like Professor Kramer, she acknowledged, "Some colleagues are mad at me for condoning the transformation."

After the presentation of the last bookstore proposal, the committee considered its conclusion and recommendations for Student Stores. It was clear to everyone on the committee that the Barnes & Noble College proposal would be chosen, as it best achieved the objectives on the committee's list. Scholarship funding would quadruple to about $1.7 million, employees would have three years of guaranteed employment, Bull's Head would increase in size from about 16,000 to 70,000 titles, and students would be guaranteed the lowest prices on textbooks. Finally, Barnes & Noble College would make a substantial investment in remodeling the store.

An exchange occurred toward the end of the last committee meeting that captures one of the main themes of this book. As Professor Kramer tells it, "We had a very short time to make the decision after the last presentation. Brad [Ives]'s approach was different from academics. He had already decided. Brad did not know how an academic community makes decisions. I said to him, 'We need time to look at this and to go around the room. What's the rush? After all this time, we need more than ten or fifteen minutes to give our feedback.' This was a cultural difference between Brad, the faculty and some of the staff. So we talked for about an hour and everyone felt they had a chance to voice their opinion." At the end of the meeting the Barnes & Noble College proposal was the one recommended.

Another cultural difference that emerged from the process was how disagreements within the committee were presented to the public. Lloyd Kramer was particularly unhappy that the university did not want any committee disagreements becoming public. He noted, "Disagreement should be seen as a positive sign of open debates, not as a PR problem."

Both Professors Taylor and Kramer praised Brad Ives's leadership of the committee. Lloyd Kramer says, "I was skeptical about Brad. I thought he was part of the new regime who did not understand our core values. But he came to understand them very clearly." Beverly Taylor adds, "Brad did a terrific job. He was very conversant with analyzing the proposals; he was on top of the business issues; and he was attentive to the feelings of faculty. He was not trying to bulldoze over our sentiments in the name of a business model."

Not everyone on campus celebrates the Student Stores transition as a resounding success. Some faculty, particularly in the arts and humanities, feel that the implementation of the new store layout, with Bull's Head located upstairs and away from foot traffic, has greatly diminished the intellectual atmosphere and impact of the bookstore. This perception persists in spite of Barnes & Noble adding tens of thousands of titles to the Bull's Head shelves.

When asked whether he thought that the new Student Stores lived up to faculty expectations, Kramer says, "I think it has. My colleagues sometimes complain about problems with textbook orders. I have not faced that problem." (Evidently, Barnes & Noble's more commercial approach to inventory management makes it difficult for students to buy textbooks after the first few weeks of the semester.) Beverly Taylor is more circumspect in her response to the outsourcing. "The school spirit part looks great and is inviting to visitors. I don't like the feel of [the overall store] . . . but it's all right. Something the faculty treasured [the old Bull's Head Bookshop] has been taken away from them. It does not seem that welcoming. It's like a Barnes & Noble store."

From the vantage point of 2018, however, the outsourcing of Student Stores has been a very successful business decision, with significant and positive implications for the university. Barnes & Noble College has fulfilled the promises made in its proposal: a great deal more money is going to student scholarships, employees have been retained, Bull's Head has a vastly greater selection, textbook prices are low, and the store has an entirely new and more contemporary look and feel, which Brad Ives describes as a "wow factor."

This case study illustrates that business and academic leaders can work together effectively on issues that are important—both financially and culturally—to universities. It also illustrates some of the challenges in doing this, because academics and businesspeople (as we have noted throughout the book) think differently about both the process of making decisions and the importance of various outcomes of these decisions. Looking into the future, all of us who care about higher education will need to collaborate successfully to preserve and to enhance the quality of the institutions that contribute so much to our prosperity and our quality of life.

Acknowledgments

This book began as an idea for an article that would explore differences between businesses and academic organizations. We are grateful to the team at Edelman who worked with Jim on the original concept. After we thought about it for nearly two years, the opportunity to write not an article but a book presented itself, and we decided to pursue it.

Our hope from the beginning was that businesspeople who want to help make universities better would benefit from the book. As discussed in this work, board members and senior university leaders (among others) who come from business will be much more effective if they understand the most important elements of how colleges and universities operate. Our sincere hope is that the book will help to preserve and enhance the excellence of American higher education by facilitating successful collaboration of business and academic leaders.

We are indebted to the many people we interviewed during the writing process. Their insights regarding what businesspeople should know about universities made the book much better. Many of these are or were in various positions at the University of North Carolina at Chapel Hill, including several current or former members of the board of trustees: Alston Gardner, Julia Grumbles, Kel Landis, Steve Lerner, Sallie Shuping-Russell, John Townsend, and Richard "Stick" Williams. We also interviewed James Moeser and Holden Thorp, two former UNC–Chapel Hill chancellors; Doug Shackelford, Jack Evans, Paul Fulton, and Steve Jones, current and former deans of the Kenan-Flagler Business School at UNC; and Bill Starling, former chair of the Kenan-Flagler Board of Visitors. Additionally, we consulted a number of UNC faculty: Penny Abernathy, Joe DeSimone, Paul Friga, Michael Jacobs, Lloyd Kramer, Charles Merritt, Ben Rosen, Beverly Taylor, and Ted Zoller. Other conversations were with people in a range of senior university leadership roles: Martin Brinkley, Susan Cates, Matt Fajack, Brad Ives, Dwayne Pinkney, Mark Merritt, and Don Rose.

Several current or former university presidents were gracious in agreeing to be interviewed: Stuart Bell (University of Alabama), Mitch Daniels (Purdue University), Richard Freeman (Northeastern University), Susan Resnick Pierce (University of Puget Sound), and Nido Qubein (High Point University). We also engaged with several current or former board members or chairs at various universities, including Frank Carroll (Fairfield University), Maria DiPietro (Suffolk University), Bill

Hawkins (Duke University), Sherry Lansing (University of California System), Tim McGinley (Purdue University), Chuck Swaboda (Marquette University), and Teresa Williams (Western Carolina University).

Other colleagues and thought leaders in higher education helped us, including Greg Bedell (Huron Consulting), Jessica Brack (Valencia Capital), Amy Burkert (Carnegie Mellon University), Trey Crabb (Morgan Stanley), Suresh Garimella (Purdue University), Andrew Hermalyn (2U), Jordan Kerner (The Kerner Entertainment Company), Byron Loflin (Center for Board Excellence), Jim Roth (Huron Consulting), Jeff Pfeffer (Stanford University Graduate School of Business), and Laurie Wilder (Parker Search).

We thank the representatives of the colleges and universities we used as examples in many parts of the book: Carnegie Mellon University (Amy Burkert and Laurie Weingart), Gonzaga University (Elisabeth Mermann-Jozwiak), Pomona College (Audrey Bilger), the U.S. Air Force Academy, the University of North Carolina at Chapel Hill, and the University of Wisconsin–Eau Claire (Jane Becker and Patricia Kleine). The book is stronger based on the information they provided.

A number of people read and provided comments on drafts of one or more chapters of the book. In addition to many of the individuals named above, we received help from Bruce Cairns, Walt Clarke, Rudi Colloredo-Mansfeld, Patrick Conway, Bridget Dean, Jan Dean, Mike Desautels, Jean Elia, Steve Farmer, Dave Hoffman, Steve Keadey, Bill Keyes, Susan King, Patricia Kleine, Charlie Mercer, Layna Moseley, Colleen O'Neill Yanchulis, Abigail Panter, Andy Perrin, Joy Renner, Terri Rhodes, Kara Simmons, Neera Skurky, Ron Strauss, and Carol Tresolini.

Many thanks go to Patricia Beeson (University of Pittsburgh) and Graham Stewart (Vanderbilt University) for their formal reviews of the entire manuscript. Their suggestions helped tremendously in improving our final draft.

We also would like to thank the team at UNC Press, including Director John Sherer, who expressed enthusiasm for the book before the first word had been written; Editorial Director Mark Simpson-Vos, who provided crucial guidance as we wrote the book; and Associate Editor Jessica Newman, who graciously helped us navigate the editing and publication process.

Tina Narron and the Executive Development and Executive MBA teams at the UNC Kenan-Flagler Business School provided office space, computer support, and encouragement (and the occasional snack) throughout the writing process. Mike Desautels and Bill Zegowitz offered the kind of unfailing support that can come only from lifelong friends.

And finally, we could not have written the book without the support of our families, to whom this book is dedicated.

Notes

ABBREVIATIONS

CHE   *Chronicle of Higher Education*
IHE   *Inside Higher Ed*
NYT   *New York Times*
UNC University of North Carolina

INTRODUCTION

1. "Fast Facts," National Center for Educational Statistics, U.S. Department of Education, 2018, accessed May 24, 2018, https://nces.ed.gov/fastfacts/display .asp?id=372.

2. Reid Wilson, "Census: More Americans Have College Degrees Than Ever Before," *The Hill*, April 3, 2017, accessed December 10, 2018, https://thehill.com /homenews/state-watch/326995-census-more-americans-have-college-degrees -than-ever-before.

3. Jennifer Ma, Matea Pender, and Meredith Welch, "College Pays 2016," College Board Trends in Higher Education Series, December 2016, accessed May 27, 2018, https://trends.collegeboard.org/sites/default/files/education-pays-2016 -full-report.pdf.

4. Throughout this book we use the terms "higher education" and "the academy" interchangeably, and we refer to postsecondary institutions generically as colleges or universities. Generally, the term "college" refers to an institution that grants only undergraduate degrees, and "university" refers to the granting of graduate and professional degrees (master's, doctorate, juris doctor, medical doctor, etc.). We explore classification of institutions in chapter 2. See also *Merriam-Webster*'s definition of the academy: "higher education—used with *the*; the functions of the academy in modern society." Accessed July 13, 2018, https:// www.merriam-webster.com/dictionary/academy.

5. Lee Gardner, "How Maine Became a Laboratory for the Future of Public Higher Ed," *CHE*, February 25, 2018, accessed February 28, 2018, https://www .chronicle.com/article/How-Maine-Became-a-Laboratory/242621.

6. Holden Thorp and Buck Goldstein, *Engines of Innovation: The Entrepreneurial University in the Twenty-First Century*, 2nd ed. (Chapel Hill: University of North Carolina Press, 2013).

7. Drew Disilver, "5 Facts about Today's College Graduates," Pew Research Center FacTank, May 30, 2014, accessed May 5, 2018, http://www.pewresearch .org/fact-tank/2014/05/30/5-facts-about-todays-college-graduates/.

8. In *How University Boards Work*, Robert A. Scott also identifies this problem and argues that the lack of knowledge is due to inadequate orientation programs for trustees. Scott, *How University Boards Work: A Guide for Trustees, Officers, and Leaders in Higher Education* (Baltimore: Johns Hopkins University Press, 2018).

9. Rick Seltzer, "Ousters on President's First Day," *IHE*, July 3, 2018, accessed July 3, 2018, https://www.insidehighered.com/news/2018/07/03/new-university -oklahoma-president-wastes-no-time-administrative-overhaul?utm_source =Inside+Higher+Ed&utm_campaign=5d9e52cd28-DNU_COPY_01&utm_medium =email&utm_term=0_1fcbc04421–5d9e52cd28–198528849&mc_cid=5d9e52cd28 &mc_eid=93352f72a0.

10. Scott Beardsley, *Higher Calling: The Rise of Nontraditional Leaders in Academia* (Charlottesville: University of Virginia Press, 2017). Beardsley spent his career at McKinsey & Company and is now a dean. See also Fernanda Zamudio-Suarez, "4 Months into His Tenure, a Flagship's President Proposes 50 Faculty Layoffs," *CHE*, May 3, 2018, accessed May 4, 2018, https://www.chronicle.com /article/4-Months-Into-His-Tenure-a/243336?cid=at&utm_source=at&utm _medium=en&elqTrackId=8474636f7e674c9da2e3464cba1c2f58&elq=229ab540 128d4c3da934fa8c8bb91cb8&elqaid=18935&elqat=1&elqCampaignId=8547.

11. Greg Toppo, "By One Measure, 'Nontraditional' Presidents Less Rare," *IHE*, May 30, 2018, accessed June 1, 2018, https://www.insidehighered.com/news/2018 /05/30/new-findings-cast-net-more-broadly-nontraditional-college-presidents ?utm_source=Inside+Higher+Ed&utm_campaign=5e05024d7e-DNU_COPY _01&utm_medium=email&utm_term=0_1fcbc04421–5e05024d7e-198528849&mc _cid=5e05024d7e&mc_eid=93352f72a0.

12. Seltzer, "Ousters on President's First Day."

13. Susan Resneck Pierce, *Governance Reconsidered: How Boards, Presidents, Administrators and Faculty Can Help Their Colleges Thrive* (San Francisco: Jossey-Bass, 2014), 20–22.

14. "Issue Brief: Federal and State Funding of Higher Education, a Changing Landscape," *Pew Charitable Trust Magazine*, June 11, 2015, accessed July 3, 2018, http://www.pewtrusts.org/en/research-and-analysis/issue-briefs/2015/06 /federal-and-state-funding-of-higher-education.

15. "Issue Brief."

16. "Public Research Universities: Changes in State Funding," Lincoln Project: Excellence and Access in Public Higher Education, American Academy of Arts

and Sciences, 2015, accessed July 3, 2018, https://www.amacad.org/publication
/public-research-universities-changes-state-funding.

17. Keith Whittington, "Free Speech Is a Core Tenet of the Academy. College
Trustees Really Ought to Know That," *CHE*, December 8, 2018, accessed
December 8, 2018, https://www.chronicle.com/article/Free-Speech-Is-a-Core
-Tenet-of/245264?cid=pm&utm_source=pm&utm_medium=en&elqTrackId=af416
36dcb654cddb77dcffc7b5fd910&elq=e9db1e5a4d224ef7b0942f79104b30b6&elqaid
=21590&elqat=1&elqCampaignId=10384.

18. Most academics would be equally in trouble if asked to serve on the board
of a business.

19. Samuel Cohen, "Scholarly Publishing's Last Stand," *CHE*, April 22, 2018,
accessed April 22, 2018, https://www.chronicle.com/article/Scholarly-Publishing
-s-Last/243187.

20. Quoted in Frederick Rudolph, *The American College and University:
A History* (New York: Alfred A. Knopf, 1962), 172.

21. Beardsley, *Higher Calling.*

22. Interview with Dean Martin Brinkley, University of North Carolina at
Chapel Hill School of Law, October 5, 2017.

23. Interview with former UNC–Chapel Hill Board of Trustees member Alston
Gardner, October 17, 2017.

24. Interview with former UNC–Chapel Hill Board of Trustees member Steve
Lerner, October 12, 2017.

25. It is ironic that while many businesspeople agonize that universities are
not more businesslike, many faculty members agonize about the encroaching
corporatization of higher education. This concern was most memorably
articulated by Derek Bok, *Universities in the Marketplace: The Commercialization
of Higher Education* (Princeton: Princeton University Press, 2003).

26. Jim Collins, *Good to Great and the Social Sectors: Why Business Thinking Is
Not the Answer* (New York: HarperCollins, 2005), 1.

27. We are indebted to Dean Martin Brinkley for this suggestion.

28. Goldie Blumenstyk, *American Higher Education in Crisis? What Everyone
Needs to Know* (New York: Oxford University Press, 2014).

CHAPTER 1

1. We are not referring to for-profit colleges, which are out of scope for this
book.

2. M. D. Cohen, J. G. March, and J. P. Olsen, "A Garbage Can Model of
Organizational Choice," *Administrative Science Quarterly* 17, no. 1 (1972): 1–25.

3. See John V. Lombardi, *How Universities Work* (Baltimore: Johns Hopkins University Press, 2013), for an extended discussion of the concept of quality as the bottom line for universities.

4. See Scott Beardsley, *Higher Calling: The Rise of Nontraditional Leaders in Academia* (Charlottesville: University of Virginia Press, 2017), for a similar discussion of this pattern. Also see Charles Clotfelter, "How Rich Universities Get Richer, and Leave Everyone Else Behind," *CHE*, October 27, 2017, accessed February 6, 2018, https://www.chronicle.com/article/How-Rich-Universities-Get /241567; and Jim Collins, *Good to Great and the Social Sectors: Why Business Thinking Is Not the Answer* (New York: HarperCollins, 2005), who considers this a variation on the "flywheel effect," p. 23.

5. Including those found in *Bloomberg BusinessWeek, Forbes, Money, Princeton Review, The Economist, Financial Times*, and the *Times Higher Education*.

6. Abram Brown, "Why Forbes Removed 4 Schools from Its America's Best Colleges Rankings," *Forbes*, August 12, 2013, accessed February 5, 2018, https:// www.forbes.com/sites/abrambrown/2013/07/24/why-forbes-removed-4-schools -from-its-americas-best-colleges-rankings/#2e4128333521. Also see John Tierney, "Your Annual Reminder to Ignore the *U.S. News & World Report* College Rankings," *The Atlantic*, September 10, 2013, accessed February 5, 2018, https:// www.theatlantic.com/education/archive/2013/09/your-annual-reminder-to -ignore-the-em-us-news-world-report-em-college-rankings/279103/; and Scott Jaschik, "Rankings Mess, Getting Worse," *IHE*, January 29, 2018, accessed February 5, 2018, https://www.insidehighered.com/admissions/article/2018/01 /29/questions-continue-arise-about-data-temple-provided-rankings-which-it. For a more forgiving analysis of the reaction of institutions to high-stakes rankings, see Wendy Nelson Espeland and Michael Sauder, "Rankings and Reactivity: How Public Measures Recreate Social Worlds," *American Journal of Sociology* 113, no. 1 (2007): 1–40, accessed February 5, 2018, https://www .researchgate.net/profile/Wendy_Espeland/publication/249176686_Rankings _and_Reactivity_How_Public_Measures_Recreate_Social_Worlds/links/55fc19d 208aeba1d9f3b1967/Rankings-and-Reactivity-How-Public-Measures-Recreate -Social-Worlds.pdf?origin=publication_detail.

7. See Jerry Muller, *The Tyranny of Metrics* (Princeton: Princeton University Press, 2018), for a somewhat parallel discussion of metrics in general and rankings in particular.

8. Patricia Beeson, personal communication, October 31, 2018.

9. An example of this sense of urgency is the CEO in the 1989 movie *National Lampoon's Christmas Vacation*, who picks up the phone and tells his assistant, "Get me somebody . . . anybody . . . and get me somebody while I'm waiting!"

10. All of this is particularly characteristic of American businesses. Compared to businesses elsewhere (especially in Asia), American businesspeople focus on the short term. See, for example, Alana Semuels, "How to Stop Short-Term Thinking at America's Companies," *The Atlantic*, December 30, 2016, accessed May 30, 2018, https://www.chronicle.com/article/Enough-With-the-Crisis -Talk-/243423.

11. Robert M. Hendrickson, Jason E. Lane, James T. Harris, and Richard H. Dorman, *Academic Leadership and Governance in Higher Education: A Guide for Trustees, Leaders, and Aspiring Leaders of Two- and Four-Year Institutions* (Sterling, Va.: Stylus Publishing, 2013). See also Randall L. Geiger, *Knowledge and Money: Research Universities and the Paradox of the Marketplace* (Palo Alto: Stanford University Press, 2004).

12. Melissa Tarrant, Nathaniel Bray, and Stephen Katsinas, "The Invisible Colleges Revisited: An Empirical Review," *Journal of Higher Education*, December 14, 2017, accessed February 6, 2018, http://www.tandfonline.com/doi/abs/10.1080 /00221546.2017.1390971. Summarized in Rick Seltzer, "Tracking Invisible Colleges," *IHE*, January 11, 2018, accessed February 6, 2018, https://www.insidehighered .com/news/2018/01/11/research-examines-changes-over-45-years-small-private -colleges.

13. Scott Jaschik, "Shocking Decision at Sweet Briar," *IHE*, March 4, 2015, accessed February 5, 2018, https://www.insidehighered.com/news/2015/03/04 /sweet-briar-college-will-shut-down; Cheryl Gay Stolberg, "Anger and Activism Greet Plan to Shut Sweet Briar College," *NYT*, March 22, 2015, accessed February 5, 2018, https://www.nytimes.com/2015/03/23/education/sweet-briars -imminent-closing-stirs-small-uprising-in-a-college-idyll.html.

14. James G. March and Johan P. Olsen, *Ambiguity and Choice in Organizations* (Oslo: Universitetforlaget, 1976).

15. All communities have their politics. Some critics have compared the dynamics of professional associations to those of middle schools, but we find this disrespectful to middle school students.

16. Many journals have a "home" at a particular university, but this home may change as the editor is replaced or changes jobs.

17. From 1948 to 1953 former Supreme Commander of Allied Forces in Europe and future president Dwight D. Eisenhower served as president of Columbia University. When faculty member Isidore Rabi won the Nobel Prize, Eisenhower observed that it was good to see university employees get such recognition, at which point Rabi interrupted the president to say, "Excuse me, sir, but the faculty are not employees of the university. The faculty are the university!" Percy Trappe, "University Humor: Dwight Eisenhower," The Academic Anchor, August 9, 2012,

accessed June 14, 2018, https://academicanchor.wordpress.com/2012/08/09 /dwight-eisenhower-and-university-faculty/.

18. There are, however, areas of research, such as laboratory safety or the treatment of human subjects, that necessarily have a high level of standardization.

19. In Walter Isaacson's biography, we learn that Leonardo da Vinci told a frustrated patron that what looks like procrastination is inherent to the creative process. Walter Isaacson, *Leonardo da Vinci* (New York: Simon and Schuster, 2017), 279–81. In fairness, few can be compared to Leonardo, "a genius undisciplined by diligence" (82); his track record of finishing projects was not good. But without him and his procrastination there would be no *Mona Lisa* or *The Last Supper*.

20. Howard Aldrich and Solvi Lillejord, "Stop Making Sense! Why Aren't Universities Better at Promoting Innovative Teaching?," in *The Social Worlds of Higher Education: Handbook for Teaching in a New Century*, ed. Bernice A. Pescosolido and Ronald Aminzade (Thousand Oaks, Calif.: Pine Forge Press, 1999), 301–8.

21. We acknowledge that training and teaching are not the same, but their differences may be due in some degree to their different settings.

22. Hendrickson et al., *Academic Leadership and Governance in Higher Education*, 29.

23. Lombardi, *How Universities Work*.

24. Muller, *The Tyranny of Metrics*, 8.

25. This transcends generations of businesses. Decades ago Avis Rental Car became famous for its apologetic "We're #2, but we try harder!" ad campaign. Many years later the name Amazon was chosen for a fledgling online book retailer partly because the name of the enormous river suggested massive size.

26. Lombardi, *How Universities Work*, 8.

27. John Warner, "ASU Is 'The New American University'—It's Terrifying," *IHE*, January 25, 2015, accessed February 6, 2018, https://www.insidehighered.com /blogs/just-visiting/asu-new-american-university-its-terrifying.

28. Ed Michaels, Helen Handfield-Jones, and Beth Axelrod, *The War for Talent* (Cambridge, Mass.: Harvard Business Press, 2001), 2. The authors report that the phrase was coined in conjunction with a study conducted by McKinsey & Co. in 1997.

29. The Talent Management Institute is held every year at the UNC Kenan-Flagler Business School.

30. "Education: View from the Bridge," *Time*, November 17, 1958. Impressively, Kerr was the source of another all-time great quote about universities: "I have

sometimes thought of the modern university as a series of individual faculty entrepreneurs held together by a common grievance over parking."

31. Again, this is a particular characteristic of American businesses. European businesses, for example, have evolved so as to give more equal emphasis to the expectations of different stakeholder groups.

32. Aristotle (in *Ethics*) wrote that "honor cannot be the highest good, because it is diminished when it is shared." Universities recognize this and would prefer to be ranked number 1 rather than be tied for the number 1 ranking. One more argument for the relevance of the humanities.

33. Henry Mintzberg, a noted management scholar, describes both types of organizations as "professional bureaucracies." Henry Mintzberg, "Organization Design: Fashion or Fit?," *Harvard Business Review*, January 1981.

CHAPTER 2

1. "The Condition of Education 2018," National Center for Educational Statistics, Department of Education, 2018, accessed May 24, 2018, https://nces .ed.gov/pubs2018/2018144.pdf.

2. Carnegie Classification 2015 Update Facts and Figures, accessed May 12, 2018, http://carnegieclassifications.iu.edu/downloads/CCIHE2015-FactsFigures.pdf.

3. Georgia (first public university to receive a charter) and North Carolina (first public university to admit and graduate students) both claim to be the oldest public university. William & Mary was founded as a private university in 1693, making it the oldest university that is currently public, but it has only been public since 1906, when it began receiving support from the Commonwealth of Virginia.

4. See also the Association of Public and Land-Grant Universities, accessed February 14, 2018, http://www.aplu.org. Chapter 4 provides more detail on the government's role in creating these universities.

5. Nathan Schneider, "The University Is Not an Aristocracy, So Why Do We Value Selectivity over Social Mobility?," *CHE*, May 20, 2018, accessed January 2, 2019, https://www.chronicle.com/article/The-University-Is-Not-an/243465. Schneider emphasizes, "Our job is not to be elite, by some contrived measure, or to outcompete the competition. It is to serve."

6. "Fast Facts," National Center for Educational Statistics, U.S. Department of Education, 2018, accessed May 12, 2018, https://nces.ed.gov/fastfacts/display.asp ?id=372.

7. UNC–Chapel Hill Mission and Values, https://www.unc.edu/about/mission/.

8. Quoted in Allison Hawkins, "Graduates-to-Be, Don't Lose Sight of the Needs of NC," *Daily Tar Heel*, April 17, 2012, accessed February 14, 2018, http://www .dailytarheel.com/index.php/article/2012/04/col_0417.

9. "Largest Universities in the United States by Enrollment," World Atlas, accessed December 19, 2017, https://www.worldatlas.com/articles/largest -universities-in-the-united-states.html. Three of the top seven institutions are in the Sunbelt states of Florida, Texas, and Arizona, reflecting recent population shifts in the United States.

10. Samantha Lindsay, "The 35 Biggest Colleges in the United States," September 1, 2017, accessed December 19, 2017, https://blog.prepscholar.com /the-biggest-colleges-in-the-united-states.

11. "Understanding College and University Endowments," American Council on Education, 2014, accessed December 19, 2017, http://www.acenet.edu/news -room/Documents/Understanding-Endowments-White-Paper.pdf.

12. "How large are the endowments of colleges and universities in the United States?," National Center for Education Statistics, accessed December 19, 2017, https://nces.ed.gov/fastfacts/display.asp?id=73.

13. "Endowment per Student for 2018," College Raptor, accessed December 19, 2017, https://www.collegeraptor.com/college-rankings/details/EndowmentPer Student.

14. "Understanding College and University Endowments." The tax bill passed in 2017, which taxes universities with endowments per student of over $500k, affected only private universities, as no public universities reached this threshold. "Final GOP Deal Would Tax Large Endowments," *IHE*, December 18, 2017, accessed December 19, 2017 https://www.insidehighered.com/news/2017/12/18 /large-endowments-would-be-taxed-under-final-gop-tax-plan.

15. Richard Vedder and Christopher Denhart, "22 Richest Schools in America," *Forbes*, July 30, 2014, accessed June 12, 2018, https://www.forbes.com/sites/ccap /2014/07/30/22-richest-schools-in-america/#6c05a1476982.

16. "State Higher Education Executive Officers, Public FTE Enrollment and Educational Appropriations per FTE, US, FY 1991–2016, Illinois and Everyone Else," *IHE*, April 20, 2017, accessed December 19, 2017, https://www.inside highered.com/news/2017/04/20/state-support-higher-education-increased -2016-not-counting-illinois.

17. "Trends in Higher Education, Average Published Undergraduate Charges by Sector and by Carnegie Classification, 2017–2018," The College Board, accessed December 19, 2017, https://trends.collegeboard.org/college-pricing/figures-tables /average-published-undergraduate-charges-sector-2017–18.

18. Stephanie Saul, "Public Colleges Chase Out-of-State Students, Tuition," *NYT*, July 7, 2016, accessed December 19, 2017, https://www.nytimes.com/2016 /07/08/us/public-colleges-chase-out-of-state-students-and-tuition.html.

19. Robert A. Scott, *How University Boards Work: A Guide for Trustees, Officers, and Leaders in Higher Education* (Baltimore: Johns Hopkins University Press, 2018), 22.

20. Marjorie Valbrun, "NACUBO Report Finds Tuition Discounting Again," *IHE*, April 30, 2018, accessed November 16, 2018, https://www.insidehighered .com/news/2018/04/30/nacubo-report-finds-tuition-discounting-again.

21. Valbrun, "NACUBO Report."

22. "Tuition Discounting," Association of Governing Boards, accessed December 10, 2018, https://www.agb.org/briefs/tuition-discounting.

23. "National University Rankings," *U.S. News & World Report*, accessed December 19, 2017, https://www.usnews.com/best-colleges/rankings/national -universities.

24. "How *U.S. News* Calculated the 2018 Best Colleges Rankings," *U.S. News & World Report*, accessed December 19, 2017, https://www.usnews.com/education /best-colleges/articles/how-us-news-calculated-the-rankings.

25. "Top Colleges Doing the Most for the American Dream," *NYT*, May 25, 2017, accessed December 17, 2017, https://www.nytimes.com/interactive/2017/05/25 /sunday-review/opinion-pell-table.html. Interestingly, institutions that are part of the University of California system occupy the first five spots on this list. This link also provides a column on university endowment per student.

26. Carnegie Classification database, accessed December 20, 2017, http:// carnegieclassifications.iu.edu/.

27. Carnegie Classification Summary Tables, accessed December 20, 2017, http://carnegieclassifications.iu.edu/downloads.php.

28. Basic Classification Description, accessed December 26, 2018, http:// carnegieclassifications.iu.edu/classification_descriptions/basic.php.

29. Greg Toppo, "Universe of Doctoral Universities Expands Carnegie: Classification's New Category of 'Doctoral/Professional Universities' Acknowledges Growing Role of Non-Research-Oriented Doctoral Work in Graduate Education," *IHE*, December 19, 2018, accessed December 26, 2018, https://www.insidehighered.com/news/2018/12/19/professional-practice-doctoral -category-expands-carnegie-system.

30. Basic Classification Description, accessed December 26, 2018.

31. Carnegie Classification 2015 Update Facts and Figures, accessed December 22, 2017, http://carnegieclassifications.iu.edu/downloads/CCIHE2015-Facts Figures.pdf.

32. "Campus History," University of Wisconsin–Eau Claire, accessed December 21, 2017, http://www.uwec.edu/about/campus-history/.

33. "United States Air Force Academy History," United States Air Force Academy, accessed February 15, 2018, http://www.usafa.af.mil/About-Us/Fact-Sheets/Display/Article/428274/air-force-academy-history/.

34. "About Gonzaga University," Gonzaga University, accessed December 21, 2017, https://www.gonzaga.edu/About/default.asp.

35. Carnegie classifications sometimes shift as institutions expand their degree offerings and number of degrees granted and as Carnegie makes adjustments to its classification process. For instance, from 2015 to 2017 Gonzaga was listed under the master's category, but in 2018 the university moved into the doctoral/professional category: "institutions with below 20 research/scholarship doctoral degrees that awarded at least 30 professional practice doctoral degrees in at least 2 programs during the update year [2018]." Basic Classification Description, accessed December 26, 2018, http://carnegieclassifications.iu.edu/classification_descriptions/basic.php.

36. The acronym WWAMI stands for the states served by the UW School of Medicine: Washington, Wyoming, Alaska, Montana and Idaho, https://www.uwmedicine.org/school-of-medicine/md-program/wwami.

37. "A Brief History of Pomona College," Pomona College, accessed December 22, 2017, https://www.pomona.edu/about/brief-history-pomona-college.

CHAPTER 3

1. These categorizations are not fixed. History may be considered as either part of humanities or social sciences; psychology is sometimes grouped with social sciences and sometimes with natural sciences. Thanks to our colleague Andy Perrin for pointing out these possibilities.

2. We once asked the head of a conservative think tank what percentage of undergraduate courses she thought was infused with liberal bias. She replied about 90 percent. We believe she was likely focused on courses in humanities and social sciences rather than in math and natural sciences or in the professional schools we discuss next. And in our experience, this is still likely an exaggeration.

3. In some cases a university has a department in the college rather than a professional school. For example, UNC–Chapel Hill's computer science department is in the College of Arts and Sciences, whereas at Carnegie Mellon computer science constitutes its own school.

4. The quotes in this list are from the respective university websites.

5. A handful of academic institutions are chartered by the federal government (e.g., the military service academies, including the United States Air Force Academy) or by Native American tribal organizations.

6. Carnegie Mellon University has no university-wide core curriculum; all degree requirements are established by the individual schools.

7. For example, Pomona College has "Breadth of Study" requirements that include (1) criticism, analysis, and contextual study of works of the human imagination, (2) social institutions and human behavior, (3) history, values, ethics, and cultural studies, (4) physical and biological sciences, (5) mathematical and formal reasoning, and (6) creation and performance of works of art and literature. See "Degree Requirements," Pomona College, 2019, accessed January 14, 2019, http://catalog.pomona.edu/content.php?catoid=28&navoid=5634.

8. "Digest of Education Statistics," National Center for Education Statistics, 2013, accessed July 5, 2018, https://nces.ed.gov/pubs2015/2015011.pdf.

9. Libby Nelson, "Master's Degrees Are as Common Now as Bachelor's Degrees Were in the '60s," *Vox*, February 7, 2017, accessed December 10, 2018, https://www.vox.com/2014/5/20/5734816/masters-degrees-are-as-common-now-as-bachelors-degrees-were-in-the-60s.

10. It is striking how many Latin plurals are found in higher education. A starter list would include curriculum/curricula, vita/vitae, honorarium/honoraria, and of course syllabus/syllabi. Some higher education insiders (not us) can even use "foci" as the plural of "focus" with a straight face. Those of you still with us may wonder about the term "curriculum vitae." According to the *Chicago Manual of Style*, while "vitae" is indeed the plural of "vita" (life), in the term that is for good reason usually abbreviated as CV, it is the genitive singular, and the phrase may be translated as "course of life" (*Chicago Manual of Style*, 16th ed., accessed July 5, 2018, https://www.chicagomanualofstyle.org/qanda/data/faq/topics/Usage/faq0126.html). QED (quod erat demonstrandum), which means, more or less, "so there."

11. This mostly is true at larger universities. Many liberal arts colleges have smaller classes, even for introductory courses.

12. Thanks to Patricia Beeson, who articulated this idea to us.

13. George D. Kuh, *High-Impact Educational Practices: What They Are, Who Has Access to Them, and Why They Matter* (Washington, D.C.: Association of American Colleges and Universities, 2008). For a summary of the book, see "High-Impact Educational Practices," Association of American Colleges & Universities, accessed April 24, 2018, https://www.aacu.org/leap/hips.

14. *The Chronicle of Higher Education* recently compiled a list of faculty who are changing education in the classroom and beyond: "Innovators: 10 Classroom Trailblazers," October 18, 2017, accessed February 16, 2018, https://www.chronicle.com/specialreport/Innovators-10-Classroom/156. See also Becky Supiano,

"Traditional Teaching Can Deepen Inequality, Can a Different Approach Fix It?,"
CHE, May 6, 2018, accessed January 2, 2019, https://www.chronicle.com/article
/Traditional-Teaching-May/243339/.

15. Marjorie Valbrun, "Maybe Not So 'High Impact'?," *IHE*, April 25, 2018,
accessed April 25, 2018, https://www.insidehighered.com/news/2018/04/25/study
-questions-whether-high-impact-practices-yield-higher-graduation-rates?utm
_source=Inside+Higher+Ed&utm_campaign=bb41ca617b-DNU20180111&utm
_medium=email&utm_term=0_1fcbc04421-bb41ca617b-198528849&mc_cid=bb41c
a617b&mc_eid=93352f72a0.

16. John N. Gardner Institute for Excellence in Undergraduate Education,
"Supporting Student Retention through Innovations in the Curriculum; First-
Year Seminars & Learning Communities," presented at the Gardner Institute
Symposium on Student Retention, June 15, 2015.

17. Paul Jaijairam, "First-Year Seminar (FYS): The Advantages That This Course
Offers," *Journal of Education and Learning* 5, no. 20 (2016): 15–23.

18. Benjamin S. Bloom, Max D. Engelhart, Edward J. Furst, Walker H. Hill,
and David R. Krathwohl, *Taxonomy of Educational Objectives: The Classification
of Educational Goals, Handbook I: Cognitive Domain* (New York: David McKay,
1956). See also L. W. Anderson and D. R. Krathwohl, eds., *A Taxonomy for
Learning, Teaching, and Assessing: A Revision of Bloom's Taxonomy of Educational
Objectives* (Boston: Allyn and Bacon, 2001).

19. Cynthia J. Brame, "Flipping the Classroom," *Vanderbilt University Center
for Teaching (2013)*, accessed November 30, 2017, http://cft.vanderbilt.edu/guides
-sub-pages/flipping-the-classroom/.

20. Sarah L. Eddy and Kelly A. Hogan, "Getting under the Hood; How and for
Whom Does Increasing Course Structure Work?," *CBE Life Science Education* 13
(2013): 453–68.

21. This study was featured in Richard Perez-Pena, "Active Role in Class Helps
Black and First-Generation College Students, Study Says," *NYT*, September 2,
2014, accessed December 1, 2017, https://www.nytimes.com/2014/09/03
/education/active-learning-study.html.

22. Joe Bandy, "What Is Service Learning or Community Engagement?,"
Vanderbilt University Center for Teaching, accessed December 1, 2017, https://cft
.vanderbilt.edu/guides-sub-pages/teaching-through-community-engagement/.

23. "Service-Learning," University of Wisconsin–Eau Claire, 2019, accessed
December 1, 2017, https://www.uwec.edu/sl/.

24. For more information on service learning, see B. Jacoby and J. Howard,
Service-Learning Essentials: Questions, Answers, and Lessons Learned (San
Francisco: Jossey-Bass, 2014).

25. Council on Undergraduate Research home page, accessed December 4, 2017, https://www.cur.org/about_cur.

26. A thorough academic overview of issues in undergraduate research and faculty mentoring is provided in a special issue of *Mentoring and Tutoring: Partnership in Learning* 23 (2015).

27. See the special issue of *Mentoring and Tutoring*.

28. Ann Lyon Ritchie, "Vacant No More: CMU Students Present Urban Development Solutions," Carnegie Mellon University, Dietrich College of Humanities and Social Sciences, January 10, 2017, accessed December 4, 2017, https://www.cmu.edu/dietrich/news/news-stories/2017/january/ehpp-vacant -lots.html.

29. Tuan Nguyen, "The Effectiveness of Online Learning: Beyond No Significant Difference and Future Horizons," *MERLOT Journal of Online Learning and Teaching* 11, no. 2 (2015): 309–19. See also "Research on the Effectiveness of Online Learning: A Compilation of Research on Online Learning," *The Future of State Universities*, September 2011, accessed December 12, 2017, https://www .immagic.com/eLibrary/ARCHIVES/GENERAL/ACPTR_US/A110923F.pdf.

30. This section draws heavily on a report by T. W. Barrett et al., "A Review of University Makerspaces," American Society for Engineering Education, 2015, accessed December 12, 2017, https://www.asee.org/public/conferences/56/papers /13209/view.

31. Mary Lou Maher and Mi Jeong Kim, "The Impact of Tangible User Interfaces on Collaborative Design," *Human-Computer Interaction* 23, no. 2 (2008): 101–37, accessed December 12, 2017, http://maryloumaher.net/Pubs /2006pdf/ASCE_TUI.pdf.

CHAPTER 4

1. Robert M. Hendrickson, Jason E. Lane, James T. Harris, and Richard H. Dorman, *Academic Leadership and Governance in Higher Education: A Guide for Trustees, Leaders, and Aspiring Leaders of Two- and Four-Year Institutions* (Sterling, Va.: Stylus Publishing, 2013), 87.

2. Hendrickson et al. have an excellent extended discussion of these interventions, as well as an overview of the role of both the federal and state governments in higher education.

3. Andrew Kneighbaum, "Perkins Loan Extension Blocked in House, Senate," *IHE*, September 29, 2017, accessed January 9, 2018, https://www.insidehighered .com/quicktakes/2017/09/29/perkins-loan extension-blocked-house-senate.

4. Elizabeth Olson, "For Profit Law School Is Cut Off from Federal Student Loans," *NYT*, January 19, 2017, accessed September 29, 2017, https://www.nytimes

.com/2017/01/19/business/dealbook/federal-student-loans-charlotte-school-of
-law.html.

5. Susannah Snider, "What to Know if Your College Loses Federal Funding," *U.S. News & World Report*, October 14, 2014, accessed January 8, 2018, https://www
.usnews.com/education/best-colleges/paying-for-college/articles/2014/10/14
/what-to-know-if-your-college-loses-federal-funding https://www.usnews.com
/education/best-colleges/paying-for-college/articles/2014/10/14/what-to-know
-if-your-college-loses-federal-funding.

6. The IPEDS website, https://nces.ed.gov/ipeds/, is a great source of information about American higher education.

7. The Department of Justice's overview of Title IX can be found at "Overview of Title IX of the Education Amendments of 1972, 20 U.S.C. A§ 1681 ET. SEQ," https://www.justice.gov/crt/overview-title-ix-education-amendments-1972-20
-usc-1681-et-seq, accessed January 5, 2018.

8. Sarah Brown and Katherine Mangan, "What You Need to Know about the Proposed Title IX Regulations," *CHE*, November 16, 2018, accessed November 16, 2018, https://www.chronicle.com/article/What-You-Need-to-Know-About/245118.

9. The 2011 letter can be found at "U.S. Department of Education Office for Civil Rights Archived Letters," https://www2.ed.gov/about/offices/list/ocr/letters
/colleague-201104.pdf. Secretary of Education Betsy DeVos proposed its withdrawal in September 2017.

10. "Secretary DeVos: Proposed Title IX Rule Provides Clarity for Schools, Support for Survivors, and Due Process Rights for All," U.S. Department of Education, November 16, 2018, accessed November 16, 2018, https://www.ed.gov
/news/press-releases/secretary-devos-proposed-title-ix-rule-provides-clarity
-schools-support-survivors-and-due-process-rights-all.

11. Statement from the National Women's Law Center (www.nwlc.org): "The proposed changes are extensive and far-reaching. If finalized, they will drastically alter students' rights and will affect almost every aspect of a school's obligation to respond to sexual harassment against students, which includes support services, investigations, and resolution procedures. These proposals will also impact all levels of our nation's educational system, resulting in changes for millions of students, from kindergarten to graduate school. For a regulation of this magnitude, interested parties need adequate time to thoroughly review the proposed changes and provide essential analysis and input."

12. Anna North, "'This Will Make Schools Less Safe': Why Betsy DeVos's Sexual Assault Rules Have Advocates Worried," *Vox*, November 16, 2018, accessed November 16, 2018, https://www.vox.com/policy-and-politics/2018/11/16
/18096736/betsy-devos-sexual-assault-harassment-title-ix.

13. Federal Coordination and Compliance Section, U.S. Department of Justice, accessed December 19, 2018, https://www.justice.gov/crt/federal-coordination -and-compliance-section-152.

14. Melanie Moran, "Study Estimates Cost of Regulatory Compliance at 13 Colleges and Universities," *Vanderbilt News*, October 19, 2015, accessed January 15, 2018, https://news.vanderbilt.edu/2015/10/19/regulatory-compliance/.

15. Jelani Cobb, "Under Trump, a Hard Test for Howard University," *New Yorker*, January 15, 2018, is an overview of the challenges faced by historically black colleges and universities in general and Howard University (a prestigious historically black school in Washington, D.C., and not a land-grant institution) in particular; accessed January 9, 2018, https://www.newyorker.com/magazine /2018/01/15/under-trump-a-hard-test-for-howard-university?elqTrackId=1f60a 502ef064d9a9d4c86863a3c0df9&elq=857b6d8b647140f495551093a4f5e69d&elqaid =17362&elqat=1&elqCampaignId=7569.

16. Meredith Hindley, "How the GI Bill Became Law in Spite of Some Veterans' Groups," *Humanities: The Magazine of the National Endowment for the Humanities*, July/August 2014, accessed January 8, 2018, https://www.neh.gov /humanities/2014/julyaugust/feature/how-the-gi-bill-became-law-in-spite -some-veterans-groups.

17. Goldie Blumenstyk, *American Higher Education in Crisis? What Everyone Needs to Know* (New York: Oxford University Press, 2014), 115.

18. Alexandra Hegji, "The Higher Education Act (HEA): A Primer," Congressional Research Service, January 2, 2014, accessed January 8, 2018, http:// www.higheredcompliance.org/resources/nps70-020614-12%20%284%29.pdf.

19. "About," Clery Center, accessed January 2, 2019, https://clerycenter.org /about-page/.

20. The annual Clery report for Carnegie Mellon can be found at Office of Title IX Initiatives, https://www.cmu.edu/title-ix/annual-security-report/index.html; and the annual Clery report for the University of Wisconsin–Eau Claire is at Clery Report and Safety Information, https://www.uwec.edu/police/resources/clery -report-safety-information/, both accessed February 11, 2019.

21. Several cases between *Plessy* and *Brown* were brought by the NAACP through its Legal Defense and Education Fund. The story of *Brown* and related cases is captured in "History—*Brown v. Board of Education* Re-enactment," United States Courts, accessed January 8, 2018, http://www.uscourts.gov /educational-resources/educational-activities/history-brown-v-board-education -re-enactment. It seems worth noting the irony (or perhaps karma?) that the plaintiff in the *Brown* case had the same surname as the justice who wrote for the majority in the *Plessy v. Ferguson* case.

22. "History—*Brown v. Board of Education* Re-enactment."

23. In their application of critical race theory to the persistence of educational outcome disparities in American public education, William F. Tate, Barbara Ladson-Billings, and Carl F. Grant suggest that "the *Brown* decision represents the Supreme Court's attempt to apply a largely mathematical solution to a social problem. The failure of the court to provide a verbal interpretation of the mathematical model it constructed left individual school districts free to develop educational responses that failed to address the needs of African-American students." William F. Tate, Barbara Ladson-Billings, and Carl F. Grant, "The *Brown* Decision Revisited: Mathematizing Social Problems," *Educational Policy* 7, no. 3 (1993), 255–75. Ladson-Billings elaborates, "I'd rather have a true *Plessy*—give me half and leave me alone—rather than a fake *Brown*" (Equity in Education Lecture Series, UNC–Chapel Hill Office of Undergraduate Retention, March 21, 2018).

24. Regents of the U. of California v. Bakke (1978), Landmark Cases of the U.S. Supreme Court, accessed January 9, 2018, http://landmarkcases.org/en/landmark /cases/regents_of_the_u_of_california_v_bakke.

25. "Affirmative Action: Court Decisions," National Conference of State Legislatures, June 2016, accessed January 8, 2018, http://www.ncsl.org/research /education/affirmative-action-court-decisions.aspx. See also Hendrickson et al., *Academic Leadership and Governance in Higher Education*, 146–49.

26. Amy Howe, "The Fisher Argument in Plain English," SCOTUSblog, October 10, 2012, accessed January 9, 2018, http://www.scotusblog.com/2012/10/the-fisher -argument-in-plain-english/.

27. Fisher v. University of Texas at Austin (Fisher II), 576 U.S. ___ (2016), American Association of University Professors, accessed January 9, 2018, https:// www.aaup.org/brief/fisher-v-university-texas-austin-fisher-ii-576-us-2016.

28. A current case involves the admissions practices of Harvard University and UNC–Chapel Hill. See Anemona Hartocollis and Stephanie Saul, "Affirmative Action Battle Has a New Focus: Asian-Americans," *NYT*, August 2, 2017, accessed January 9, 2018, https://www.nytimes.com/2017/08/02/us/affirmative-action -battle-has-a-new-focus-asian-americans.html?smid=pl-share.

29. "FAQ," Students for Fair Admissions, accessed January 2, 2019, https:// studentsforfairadmissions.org/faq/.

30. Private colleges and universities are not subject to these constitutional requirements because these institutions are not state actors. However, many private schools extend the equivalent of these rights through their policies and procedures.

31. Hendrickson et al., *Academic Leadership and Governance in Higher Education*, 144–46. The *Dixon* case was decided in U.S. federal court.

32. See Erwin Chemerinsky and Howard Gillman, *Free Speech on Campus* (New Haven: Yale University Press, 2017), for a comprehensive discussion of free speech issues. Chapter 5 is a particularly good reference for academic leaders. See also "Speech on Campus," American Civil Liberties Union, accessed January 10, 2018, https://www.aclu.org/other/speech-campus. See also "Campus Rights," Foundation for Individual Rights on Campus, accessed January 10, 2018, https://www.thefire.org/campus-rights/.

33. These provisions do not apply to private colleges and universities. However, given the universal standards for tenure and academic freedom, many private institutions have campus policies protecting free speech.

34. Caroline Simon, "Free Speech Isn't Free: It's Costing College Campuses Millions," *Forbes*, November 17, 2017, accessed January 10, 2018, https://www.forbes.com/sites/carolinesimon/2017/11/20/free-speech-isnt-free-its-costing-college-campuses-millions/#3199570b1ee7. See also Nick Roll, "Congress Rallies around Campus Free Speech," *IHE*, October 27, 2017, accessed January 10, 2018, https://www.insidehighered.com/news/2017/10/27/senate-hearing-explores-free-speech-college-campuses.

35. "May Schools Limit the Time, Place and Manner of Student Expression?," First Amendment Schools, accessed January 10, 2018, http://www.firstamendmentschools.org/freedoms/faq.aspx?id=12993.

36. *Brandenburg v. Ohio* (1969), accessed February 9, 2019, https://www.aclu.org/other/speech-campus.

37. Samantha Harris, "Misunderstanding Harassment," Foundation for Individual Rights in Education, October 16, 2012, accessed January 11, 2018, https://www.thefire.org/misunderstanding-harassment/.

38. Chemerinsky and Gillman, *Free Speech on Campus*, 82.

39. "Spotlight on Speech Codes 2018: The State of Free Speech on Our Nation's Campuses," Foundation for Individual Rights in Education, accessed January 12, 2018, https://www.thefire.org/spotlight-on-speech-codes-2018/.

40. Chemerinsky and Gillman, *Free Speech on Campus*, 52.

41. Hendrickson et al., *Academic Leadership and Governance in Higher Education*, 124.

42. Hendrickson et al. provide a thorough overview of different types of systems and boards.

43. John V. Lombardi, *How Universities Work* (Baltimore: Johns Hopkins University Press), 2013, 161.

44. Association of Governing Boards of Universities and Colleges, *Policies, Practices, and Composition of Governing Boards of Public Colleges, Universities, and Systems* (Washington, D.C.: AGB Press, 2010).

45. Interestingly, some states provide funding to private universities. Hendrickson et al., *Academic Leadership and Governance in Higher Education*, 131.

46. John Marcus, "Long-Neglected Maintenance Threatens to Further Escalate the Cost of College," The Hechinger Report, July 25, 2016, accessed January 11, 2018, http://hechingerreport.org/long-neglected-maintenance-threatens-to -further-escalate-the-cost-of-college/.

47. "Higher Education Restructuring," University of Virginia, accessed January 11, 2018, http://www.virginia.edu/restructuring/legislation.html.

48. Hendrickson et al., *Academic Leadership and Governance in Higher Education*, 127. See also Jerry Muller, *The Tyranny of Metrics* (Princeton: Princeton University Press, 2018), for a critical review of this trend.

49. FERPA (Family Educational Rights and Privacy Act) protects student privacy and is analogous to HIPAA in health care. United States Department of Education Laws and Guidance, accessed February 15, 2019, https://www2.ed.gov /policy/gen/guid/fpco/ferpa/index.html.

50. Lombardi, *How Universities Work*, 169.

51. "Accreditation: Universities and Higher Education," U.S. Department of Education, accessed January 15, 2018, https://www.ed.gov/accreditation.

52. These six organizations, along with another that accredits community colleges, are members of the Council on Higher Education Accreditation, accessed May 13, 2018, http://www.chea.org/. See also "Regional Accreditation," Wikipedia, accessed January 15, 2018, https://en.wikipedia.org/wiki/Regional _accreditation, for a map of which accrediting organizations operate in which states.

53. These standards are not without their critics. Lombardi, in *How Universities Work*, writes that "accreditation, originally invented to identify fraudulent institutions and programs, has become a defender of education fads" (156).

54. Scott Hempling, "'Regulatory Capture': Sources and Solutions," Emory Corporate Governance and Accountability Review, accessed January 15, 2018, http://law.emory.edu/ecgar/content/volume-1/issue-1/essays/regulatory-capture .html.

55. Lombardi, *How Universities Work*, 156.

56. In light of the diminished prospects of local newspapers in general and one in particular, a faculty colleague often threatened to write a letter to the editor that began, "Several decades from now, we know [our university] will remain a respected and vibrant institution. We wish we could say the same about your newspaper."

57. Robert M. Gates, *A Passion for Leadership: Lessons on Change and Reform from Fifty Years of Public Service* (New York: Alfred A. Knopf, 2016), 152–54. At the intersection of alumni, sports fans, and social media, there is a constant storm of commentary that is impressive in its scope and intensity. If you are not familiar with this phenomenon, take any university with a top basketball team that wears blue (there are at least four), and see for yourself. Caveat lector.

CHAPTER 5

1. Thanks to Patricia Beeson, who articulated this idea to us.

2. Aaron Clauset, Samuel Argesman, and Daniel B. Larremore, "Systematic Inequality and Hierarchy in Faculty Hiring Networks," *Science Advances* 1, no. 1 (2015), accessed February 15, 2018, http://advances.sciencemag.org/content /advances/1/1/e1400005.full.pdf.

3. Neil G. Ruiz, *The Geography of Foreign Students in U.S. Higher Education: Origins and Destinations* (Washington, D.C.: Global Cities Initiative: A Joint Project of Brookings and JP Morgan Chase, 2014).

4. John V. Lombardi, *How Universities Work* (Baltimore: Johns Hopkins University Press, 2013), makes this connection explicit, referring to academic disciplines as guilds.

5. In some departments students are actually admitted to a specific research project or lab, so this sorting-out process is already done during the admissions process.

6. "Scholarship of Teaching and Learning," UNC–Chapel Hill Center for Faculty Excellence, accessed May 13, 2018, https://cfe.unc.edu/teaching-and-learning/.

7. The equivalent of an academic résumé is a curriculum vitae. The key difference between a CV and a résumé is length. CVs almost always have two or more pages and "include information on a candidate's academic background, including teaching experience, degrees, research, awards, publications, presentations, and other achievements. CVs are ... longer than resumés, and include more information, particularly details related to one's academic background." Alison Doyle, "The Difference between a Resume and a Curriculum Vitae," *The Balance Careers*, May 8, 2018, accessed May 13, 2018, https://www .thebalancecareers.com/cv-vs-resume-2058495. See also the recent story of the University of Montana president who did not know the difference between a CV and résumé. Dan Brooks, "Seth Bodnar Suffers Academic Culture Shock," *Missoula Independent*, March 1, 2018, accessed May 13, 2018, http://missoulanews .com/opinion/brooks-seth-bodnar-suffers-academic culture-shock/article _f8d93348-1cc9-11e8-9f81-03fcd880e686.html.

8. Joel Warner and Aaron Clauset, "The Academy's Dirty Secret," *Slate*, February 2015, accessed February 15, 2018, http://www.slate.com/articles/life/education/2015/02/university_hiring_if_you_didn_t_get_your_ph_d_at_an_elite_university_good.html.

9. Vimal Patel, "Amid Professors' 'Doom-and-Gloom Talk,' Humanities Ph.D. Applications Drop," *CHE*, September 28, 2017, accessed February 15, 2018, https://www.chronicle.com/article/Amid-Professors-/241311.

10. Sarah Brown, "She Wrote a Farewell Letter to Colleagues. Then 80,000 People Read It," *CHE*, February 15, 2018, accessed February 15, 2018, https://www.chronicle.com/article/She-Wrote-a-Farewell-Letter-to/242564.

11. See also Leonard Cassuto, *The Graduate School Mess: What Caused It and How We Can Fix It* (Cambridge, Mass.: Harvard University Press, 2015).

12. Alia Wong, "Graduate School Can Have Terrible Effects on People's Mental Health," *The Atlantic*, November 27, 2018, accessed November 30, 2018, https://www.theatlantic.com/education/archive/2018/11/anxiety-depression-mental-health-graduate-school/576769/.

13. This seems like a good place to mention that human resource policies for faculty in private institutions are determined by the senior leadership and the board of trustees. In public institutions, however, faculty are generally considered state employees, and policies and practices must conform to state regulations. Many academic leaders chafe at the restrictions that this imposes in, for example, hiring and setting salaries.

14. Most universities have formalized structure around specific faculty levels and job titles. "Faculty Ranks, Appointment Tracking, and Working Title Guidelines," University of North Carolina at Chapel Hill, accessed May 13, 2018, https://academicpersonnel.unc.edu/faculty-policies-procedures-guidelines/faculty-appointments/.

15. New tenure-track hires who have not finished their dissertations (sometimes referred to as ABD or "all but dissertation") are occasionally given a temporary faculty status such as lecturer until they finish.

16. Teaching effectiveness, the evidence of which is frequently measured via student course evaluations, is increasingly important in tenure decisions at research universities, with most R1 institutions having some minimum teaching expectations for tenure and promotion.

17. Anne Boring, Kellie Ottoboni, and Phillip B. Stark, "Student Evaluations of Teaching (Mostly) Do Not Measure Teaching Effectiveness," *ScienceOpen Research*, January 7, 2016, accessed May 13, 2018, https://www.math.upenn.edu/~pemantle/active-papers/Evals/stark2016.pdf.

18. As we discussed in chapter 1, prestige is an important goal in higher education; it matters where doctoral students are hired.

19. A business friend recently suggested that people go into academics because of the absence of risk. But betting roughly fifteen years of one's professional life (the PhD program and the pre-tenure years) on a tenure decision seems pretty risky to us.

20. Dave Levinthal, "Why the Koch Brothers Are Funding Higher Education," *The Atlantic*, October 30, 2015, accessed May 13, 2018, https://www.theatlantic .com/education/archive/2015/10/spreading-the-free-market-gospel/413239/.

21. "1940 Statement of Principles on Academic Freedom and Tenure," American Association of University Professors, accessed January 2, 2019, www .aaup.org/report/1940-statement-principles-academic-freedom-and-tenure.

22. The 1915 AAUP document emerged from a meeting in Washington, D.C., on December 31, 1915, and January 1, 1916. A meeting on those dates would be a tough sell in the current academic environment, unless the meeting was held in a tropical location with colorful drinks and tiny umbrellas involved.

23. Keith Whittington, "Free Speech Is a Core Tenet of the Academy. College Trustees Really Ought to Know That," *CHE*, December 8, 2018, accessed December 8, 2018, https://www.chronicle.com/article/Free-Speech-Is-a-Core -Tenet-of/245264?cid=pm&utm_source=pm&utm_medium=en&elqTrackId=af41b 36dcb654cddb77dc11c7b5fd910&elq=e9db1e5a4d224ef7b0942f79104b30b6&elqaid =21590&elqat=1&elqCampaignId=10384.

24. "1940 Statement of Principles on Academic Freedom and Tenure," 14.

25. "1940 Statement of Principles on Academic Freedom and Tenure," 14.

26. Chris Buddle explains, "The life of an academic is not stress-free and is not all tweed-jackets, and hobnobbing at the Faculty club"; see "Why Professors Can't Relax (Even If It Will Make Us More Productive)," *Arthropod Ecology*, February 11, 2013, accessed May 13, 2018, https://arthropodecology.com/2013/02/11/why -professors-cant-relax-even-if-it-will-make-us-more productive/.

27. "UNC School of Medicine Announces Three New Sarah Graham Kenan Distinguished Professors," University of North Carolina, March 2018, accessed May 13, 2018, http://news.unchealthcare.org/news/2018/march/unc-school-of -medicine-announces-three-new-sarah-graham-kenan-distinguished-professors.

28. "Three Professors Earn Highest Faculty Distinction," Carnegie Mellon University News, May 13, 2016, accessed May 13, 2018, https://www.cmu.edu/news /stories/archives/2016/may/university-professors.html.

29. "Faculty Ranks, Appointment Tracking, and Working Title Guidelines."

30. "An Anonymous Instructor Describes 25 Years Working as an Adjunct.

Treadmill to Oblivion," *IHE*, May 11, 2015, accessed May 13, 2018, https://www
.insidehighered.com/advice/2015/05/11/essay-instructor-who-has-taught
-adjunct-25-years.

31. Goldie Blumenstyk, *American Higher Education in Crisis? What Everyone Needs to Know* (New York: Oxford University Press, 2014), 44.

32. For an overview of budgeting methods, see 6 Alternative Budgeting Methods for Colleges and Universities, *Hanover Research*, April 19, 2013, accessed June 1, 2018, https://www.hanoverresearch.com/insights-blog/6-alternative -budget-models-for-colleges-and-universities/.

33. We discuss in chapter 7 what they do with the rest of their time.

34. In some schools, such as medicine, twelve-month salaries are more common.

35. Wong, "Graduate School Can Have Terrible Effects."

36. Patricia Beeson, personal communication, October 31, 2018.

CHAPTER 6

1. "Education Department Establishes Enhanced Federal Aid Participation Requirements for ACICS-Accredited Colleges," U.S. Department of Education, December 12, 2016, accessed May 13, 2018, https://www.ed.gov/news/press -releases/education-department-establishes-enhanced-federal-aid-participation -requirements-acics-accredited-colleges.

2. Robert M. Gates, *A Passion for Leadership* (New York: Alfred A. Knopf, 2016), 8.

3. Scott Beardsley, *Higher Calling: The Rise of Nontraditional Leaders in Academia* (Charlottesville: University of Virginia Press, 2017), 191.

4. Gary A. Olson, "Exactly What Is 'Shared Governance'?" *CHE*, July 23, 2009.

5. Jim Collins, *Good to Great and the Social Sectors: Why Business Thinking Is Not the Answer* (New York: HarperCollins, 2005), 9.

6. There is not a great deal of difference between public and private institutions in the organization of academics. The differences are rather driven by size: larger institutions will have more faculty, more departments, more centers, and generally more administrative complexity.

7. Robert M. Hendrickson, Jason E. Lane, James T. Harris, and Richard H. Dorman, *Academic Leadership and Governance in Higher Education: A Guide for Trustees, Leaders, and Aspiring Leaders of Two- and Four-Year Institutions* (Sterling, Va.: Stylus Publishing, 2013), 278.

8. Howard Aldrich and Solvi Lillejord, "Stop Making Sense! Why Aren't Universities Better at Promoting Innovative Teaching?," in *The Social Worlds of Higher Education: Handbook for Teaching in a New Century*, ed. Bernice A.

Pescosolido and Ronald Aminzade (Thousand Oaks, Calif.: Sage Publishing, 1999), 301–8.

9. John V. Lombardi, *How Universities Work* (Baltimore: Johns Hopkins University Press, 2013), 8.

10. This self-supporting budget model is also referred to as ETOB: every tub on its own bottom. We discuss this and other budget models in chapter 8. See also "Harvard Explained," *Harvard Crimson*, October 4, 2002, accessed May 13, 2018, https://www.thecrimson.com/article/2002/10/24/harvard-explained-where-does -the-phrase/.

11. In their classic book, simply called *Organizations* (Cambridge, Mass.: Wiley, 1958), James March and Herbert Simon point out that, however powerful incentives may be in shaping behavior, the allocation of attention is often a sufficient explanation for what people in organizations choose to do.

12. In coal mines, when someone leaves the union bargaining unit to become a first-level supervisor, or "face boss," miners refer to that person as having "gone bossin'." While we have never heard this term used in academics, the feeling is about the same. In fact, at the University of Massachusetts–Dartmouth, the faculty union is as of this writing attempting to kick department heads out of the bargaining unit. Colleen Flaherty, "UMass–Dartmouth Wants to Boot Chairs from Union," *IHE*, June 12, 2018, accessed June 12, 2018, https://www.insidehighered. com/quicktakes/2018/06/12/umass-dartmouth-wants-boot-chairs-union?utm _source=Inside+Higher+Ed&utm_campaign=5db6c1c025-DNU_COPY_01&utm _medium=email&utm_term=0_1fcbc04421–5db6c1c025-198528849&mc_cid=5db 6c1c025&mc_eid=93352f72a0.

13. Fritz J. Roethlisberger, "The Foreman: Master and Victim of Double Talk," *Harvard Business Review*, September 1945. Accessed January 24, 2018, https://hbr .org/1965/09/the-foreman-master-and-victim-of-double-talk.

14. Olson, "Exactly What Is 'Shared Governance'?" See also Claire E. Sterk and James W. Wagner, "A Common Meaning of Faculty Governance," Emory University Academic Exchange, Spring 2014, accessed January 26, 2018, http:// www.emory.edu/ACAD_EXCHANGE/issues/2014/Spring/stories/sterkwagner /index.html.

15. Goldie Blumenstyk, *American Higher Education in Crisis? What Everyone Needs to Know* (New York: Oxford University Press, 2014), 99.

16. Olson, "Exactly What Is 'Shared Governance'?"

17. "Shared Governance," American Association of University Professors, accessed January 24, 2018, https://www.aaup.org/our-programs/shared -governance.

18. All quotes are from *Statement on Government of Colleges and Universities*,

American Association of University Professors, 1966, accessed January 24, 2018, https://www.aaup.org/report/statement-government-colleges-and-universities.

19. William Tierney and James T. Minor, *Challenges for Governance: A National Report* (Los Angeles: Center for Higher Education Policy Analysis, 2003). Accessed January 24, 2018, https://files.eric.ed.gov/fulltext/ED482060.pdf.

20. Olson, "Exactly What Is 'Shared Governance'?," makes this last point particularly well.

21. Ricky L. Jones, "U of L Faculty Offended by 'Spit in Your Face' Approach in Presidential Search," *Courier-Journal*, November 29, 2017, accessed January 26, 2017, https://www.courier-journal.com/story/opinion/columnists/ricky-jones /2017/11/29/uofl-faculty-search-president/903660001/. This article, while unusually strong in tone, captures the feelings of many faculty about corporatization in university leadership.

22. Hendrickson et al., *Academic Leadership and Governance in Higher Education*, provide a helpful overview of faculty senates, 274–77.

23. "University Senate," University of Wisconsin–Eau Claire, accessed January 25, 2018, https://www.uwec.edu/usenate/.

24. "Faculty Handbook 2017–18," Pomona College, accessed January 25, 2018, https://www.pomona.edu/sites/default/files/faculty-handbook.pdf.

25. "Faculty Handbook, Section Two, Committees of the University," Gonzaga University, accessed January 26, 2018, https://www.gonzaga.edu/-/media /Website/Documents/Academics/Academic-Vice-President/FacultyHandbook section200-0713.ashx?la=en&hash=C9F2661A2C51FF47F3109BE0108AE9388218 EF34.

26. "Governance," United States Air Force Academy, accessed May 13, 2018, https://www.usafa.edu/about/governance/.

27. "Faculty Senate," Carnegie Mellon University, accessed January 24, 2018, https://www.cmu.edu/faculty-senate/.

28. Gates, *Passion for Leadership*, 35.

29. "European Works Councils," European Trade Union Institute, accessed January 26, 2018, https://www.worker-participation.eu/European-Works -Councils.

30. Blumenstyk, *American Higher Education in Crisis?*, 99.

31. Gates, *Passion for Leadership*, 42.

32. Blumenstyk, *American Higher Education in Crisis?*, 99.

33. Larry G. Gerber, *The Rise and Decline of Faculty Governance: Professionalism and the Modern American University* (Baltimore: Johns Hopkins University Press, 2014).

34. Benjamin Ginsberg, *The Fall of the Faculty: The Rise of the All-Administrative University and Why It Matters* (New York: Oxford University Press, 2011).

35. Percy Trappe, "University Humor: Dwight Eisenhower," The Academic Anchor, August 9, 2012, accessed June 14, 2018, https://academicanchor .wordpress.com/2012/08/09/dwight-eisenhower-and-university-faculty/.

36. This absence of students in figure 6.4 is not meant to imply anything about their importance, although their absence from the model is not coincidental. Students also are not included in the organizational charts in figures 6.1 and 6.2.

37. Olson, "Exactly What Is 'Shared Governance'?"

38. Ginsberg, *Fall of the Faculty*, 164.

39. This idea was suggested to us by former UNC–Chapel Hill board member Alston Gardner. Exploration of the relationship between language and cognition can be found in an article by Bernard Comrie, called "Language and Thought," Linguistic Society of America, accessed January 26, 2018, https://www.linguistic society.org/resource/language-and-thought.

CHAPTER 7

1. Readers wanting more detail may be interested in Jonathan R. Cole's *Great American University: Its Rise to Preeminence, Its Indispensable National Role, Why It Must Be Protected* (New York: Public Affairs, 2009) or Louis Menand and Paul Ritter's *Rise of the Research University: A Sourcebook* (Chicago: University of Chicago Press, 2017).

2. Faculty in the humanities tend to use the term "scholarship" rather than "research" to describe their work.

3. Google Scholar is a tool used by academics to find scholarly research on a topic, as well as to see how often their own work has been cited.

4. Thanks to Professor Abigail Panter of UNC–Chapel Hill for help in developing this example.

5. Thanks to Professor Barbara Entwisle of UNC–Chapel Hill for suggesting this point.

6. Statistics and quotes in this section are from the National Institutes of Health website, accessed on March 9, 2018, https://www.nih.gov.

7. Some programs have abandoned deadlines, and proposals can be submitted at any time.

8. Maggie Kuo, "Relatively Few NIH Grantees Get Lion's Share of Agency's Funding," *Science*, July 18, 2017, accessed March 12, 2018, http://www.sciencemag .org/news/2017/07/relatively-few-nih-grantees-get-lion-s-share-agency-s -funding.

9. Nicholas Weiler, "UCSF Is Top Public Recipient of NIH Research Funding for 6th Consecutive Year," University of California, San Francisco News Center, March 19, 2017, accessed March 12, 2018, https://www.ucsf.edu/news/2017/03/406096 /ucsf-top-public-recipient-nih-research-funding-6th-consecutive-year.

10. Statistics and quotes in this section are from the National Science Foundation website, accessed March 9, 2018, https://www.nsf.gov.

11. While NIH grants include only direct costs, NSF grant amounts also include indirect costs, so the differences between the average grant amounts are larger than they appear.

12. National Endowment for the Arts website, accessed January 2, 2019, www .arts.gov.

13. David Hajdu, "Who Needs the NEA and the NEH? What Is Really Lost When We Cut Public Funds for the Arts and Humanities," *The Nation*, April 7, 2017, accessed December 23, 2018, https://www.thenation.com/article/who-needs -the-nea-and-neh/.

14. National Endowment for the Humanities website, accessed January 2, 2019, www.neh.gov.

15. "Funding the Arts," National Endowment for the Arts, accessed January 2, 2019, https://www.arts.gov/infographic-nea-funding-the-arts.

16. "Appropriations History," National Endowment for the Arts, accessed January 2, 2019, https://www.arts.gov/open-government/national-endowment -arts-appropriations-history.

17. "NEH and NEA Support New Higher Education Study on Integration of STEM with Arts and Humanities," NEA, July 26, 2016, accessed December 23, 2018, https://www.arts.gov/news/2016/neh-and-nea-support-new-higher -education-study-integration-stem-arts-and-humanities.

18. Jeffrey Mervis, "Data Check: U.S. Government Share of Basic Research Funding Falls below 50%," *Science*, March 9, 2017, accessed March 9, 2018, http:// www.sciencemag.org/news/2017/03/data-check-us-government-share-basic -research-funding-falls-below-50.

19. For more detail on F&A, see "7.3 Direct Costs and Facilities and Administrative Costs," NIH Grants Policy Statement, accessed March 9, 2018, https://grants.nih.gov/grants/policy/nihgps/html5/section_7/7.3_direct_costs _and_facilities_and_administrative_costs.htm. The explanation from the NSF, simply called "Indirect Cost Rates," is at https://www.nsf.gov/bfa/dias/caar /indirect.jsp, accessed March 9, 2018.

20. "Carnegie Mellon University, Foundation Indirect Cost Policies as of 5/1/14," *Foundation Relations*, accessed March 12, 2018, https://www.document cloud.org/documents/1198059-foundationindirectcosts-may14-1.html.

21. Sarah Boon, "21st Century Science Overload," *Canadian Science Publishing Blog*, January 7, 2016, accessed March 12, 2018, http://www.cdnsciencepub.com /blog/21st-century-science-overload.aspx.

22. It is worth mentioning that active researchers are likely to have several manuscripts in various stages of readiness for publication at any one time. It may therefore be weeks or even months before they return to a manuscript that has received a request for revision. Sometimes the demands of reviewers seem sufficiently difficult to meet such that the researcher gives up on one journal and submits the paper to another.

23. Given the stakes of these decisions, and the perception that they are largely out of the control of the authors, there is a dark vein of humor among academics regarding the publication process. Somehow "Reviewer 2" has taken a starring role in this show. If you're game, go to the Twitter account @AcademicsSay, which posted "Relationship goals: Acceptance, with minor revisions."

24. Faculty at prestigious institutions dominate the more prestigious journals, while faculty at less prestigious institutions more often publish in less prestigious journals; this is despite the "blind" nature of the review process, where the reviewers are not told the identity of the authors. This is partly due to the academic sorting-out process that brings stronger researchers to more prestigious universities and partly to the many advantages (including funding and networks) offered by top universities, another example of the observation in chapter 1 that the rich get richer.

25. Florida State University recently canceled its "bundle" deal with Elsevier, a major journal publisher. Other universities are considering taking this step. See Lindsay McKenzie, "Florida State Cancels Bundled Journal Deal with Elsevier," *IHE*, April 26, 2018, accessed June 1, 2018, https://www.insidehighered.com /quicktakes/2018/04/26/florida-state-cancels-bundled-journal-deal-elsevier.

26. For an extended and passionate argument in favor of the former, see Jerry Muller, *The Tyranny of Metrics* (Princeton: Princeton University Press, 2018).

27. Muller, *Tyranny of Metrics*.

28. In chapter 8 we explore the notion of "administrative bloat" and how it allegedly contributes to rising costs in higher education. Expansion of the research enterprise, as well as costs related to research compliance and reporting requirements, contributes greatly to increasing administrative costs at universities.

29. The University of Michigan Library, Research Impact Metrics, Citation Analysis, H-Index Overview, accessed March 13, 2018, http://guides.lib.umich .edu/c.php?g=282982&p=1887449.

30. Similar calculations are used to assess the impact of journals.

31. Believe it or not, this discussion still has not fully explored the complexity of assessing research. Research evaluators have to make decisions about whether research done with coauthors is as valuable as research done alone (or with uncredited graduate students). When there are coauthors, what does the order of authorship (i.e., whose name appears first) mean, if anything? The answer to these questions is different in different academic disciplines and at different institutions. Moreover, in promotion and tenure decisions, decision makers give serious consideration to letters from scholars at other institutions who may or may not be clear about their use of metrics and exercise of judgment.

32. Holden Thorp and Buck Goldstein, *Engines of Innovation: The Entrepreneurial University in the Twenty-First Century*, 2nd ed. (Chapel Hill: University of North Carolina Press, 2013). See also Don Rose and Cam Patterson, *Research to Revenue: A Practical Guide to University Start-Ups* (Chapel Hill: University of North Carolina Press, 2016).

33. The Bayh-Dole Act, passed in 1980, drastically changed technology transfer at universities by "enabling universities to retain title to inventions and take the lead in patenting and licensing groundbreaking discoveries." "Landmark Law Helped Universities Lead the Way," AUTM (Association of University Technology Managers), accessed December 19, 2018, https://autm.net/about-tech-transfer/advocacy/legislation/bayh-dole-act.

34. These points are based on an interview with Don Rose, April 18, 2018.

35. See Rose and Patterson, *Research to Revenue*, for an extended discussion of these issues.

36. See Rose and Patterson, chapter 1. See also "Bayh-Dole Act at a Glance," University of Pittsburgh Innovation Institute, accessed March 22, 2018, http://www.innovation.pitt.edu/resource/bayh-dole-act-at-a-glance/.

37. Thorp and Goldstein, *Engines of Innovation*, 34.

38. Scott Shane, *Academic Entrepreneurship: University Spinoffs and Wealth Creation* (Cheltenham, UK: Edward Elgar, 2004).

39. Dante Di Gregorio and Scott Shane, "Why Do Some Universities Generate More Start-Ups Than Others?," *Research Policy* 32 (2003): 209–27, accessed March 22, 2018, https://pdfs.semanticscholar.org/7e75/71881f8ce7fba17266d91dce16fe714d302c.pdf.

40. Thanks to Don Rose for these examples and insights.

41. "Spyryx Biosciences Secures Series A Financing," University of North Carolina, accessed April 25, 2018, http://news.unchealthcare.org/som-vital-signs/2015/may-14/uncs-spyryx-biosciences-secures-series-a-financing.

42. See the company's website for more detail: http://spyryxbio.com.

43. The Association of Public and Land-Grant Universities recognizes more

than sixty institutions that demonstrate an ongoing commitment to economic and community development through knowledge creation and applied research via its Commission on Innovation and Economic Prosperity Universities Program, accessed January 2, 2019, http://www.aplu.org/projects-and-initiatives/economic-development-and-community-engagement/innovation-and-economic-prosperity-universities-designation-and-awards-program/index.html.

44. Cole, *Great American University*, 230.

CHAPTER 8

1. "Universities Face Another Year of Low Net Tuition Revenue Growth, Survey Shows," Moody's Investors Service, November 29, 2016, accessed April 30, 2018, http://www.chronicle.com/blogs/ticker/files/2016/11/2016-Tuition-Revenue-Survey-Shows-Another-Year-of-Low-Net-Tuition-Revenue-Growth.pdf.

2. Melissa Korn, "Private Colleges Dole Out Scholarships to Boost Enrollment, but It Isn't Working," *Wall Street Journal*, April 30, 2018, accessed May 1, 2018, https://www.wsj.com/articles/private-colleges-dole-out-scholarships-to-boost-enrollment-but-it-isnt-working-1525060860.

3. Goldie Blumenstyk, *American Higher Education in Crisis? What Everyone Needs to Know* (New York: Oxford University Press, 2014), 46.

4. We have not identified the specific universities because, while the data for individual universities is technically public, it was not shared with the understanding that it would be publicly identified as coming from these universities.

5. We did not include endowment income because different universities treat it very differently in their financial reports.

6. *Financial Report 2017*, Carnegie Mellon University, accessed April 27, 2018, https://www.cmu.edu/annual-report-2017/annual_report_2017.pdf. We have excluded other sources of revenue (e.g., auxiliaries, investment income) for comparability purposes.

7. *Financial Report 2016–17*, Gonzaga University, accessed April 27, 2018, https://www.gonzaga.edu/-/media/Website/Documents/About/Offices-and-Services/Finance-Office/gufinancialreport2017.ashx?la=en&hash=06B28570365C3DFB6F84AF674D41E7C1256683C6.

8. *Audited Financial Statements for the Year Ended June 30, 2017*, Pomona College, accessed April 27, 2018, https://www.pomona.edu/sites/default/files/college-financial-statements-2017.pdf.

9. Blumenstyk, *American Higher Education in Crisis?*, 43.

10. For an overview of budgeting methods, see "6 Alternative Budgeting Methods for Colleges and Universities," *Hanover Research*, April 19, 2013, accessed

June 1, 2018, https://www.hanoverresearch.com/insights-blog/6-alternative
-budget-models-for-colleges-and-universities/.

11. "Exploring Alternative Budget Models," Education Advisory Board, 2013, accessed April 27, 2018, https://www.kpu.ca/sites/default/files/President /Exploring-Alternative-Budget-Models.pdf. See also K. Green, S. Jaschik, and D. Lederman, "The 2011 Inside Higher Ed Survey of College and University Business Officers," *IHE*, July 5, 2011, accessed April 27, 2018, https://www.inside highered.com/sites/default/server_files/files/insidehigheredcfosurveyfinal7-5 -11.pdf.

12. "Responsibility Center Management," Drexel University, accessed April 27, 2018, http://drexel.edu/rcm/approach/why/.

13. "Harvard Explained," *Harvard Crimson*, October 4, 2002, accessed May 13, 2018, https://www.thecrimson.com/article/2002/10/24/harvard-explained-where -does-the-phrase/.

14. "Budget Season Springs Again," Vanderbilt University, *Open Dore* (the provost's newsletter), March 2018, accessed April 27, 2018, https://wp0.vanderbilt .edu/email-creator/2018/03/march-2018-issue-of-the-open-dore/.

15. Some campuses, such as Duke University and UNC–Chapel Hill, having existed for more than 200 years, still have buildings named for controversial historical figures. For example, see "Julian Shakespeare Carr — Carr Building," *Names in Brick and Stone: Histories from UNC's Built Landscape*, UNC–Chapel Hill, accessed January 2, 2019, http://unchistory.web.unc.edu/building-narratives /julian-shakespeare-carr-carr-building/.

16. "Most endowments are designed to keep the principal corpus intact so it can grow over time, but allow the nonprofit to use the annual investment income for programs, or operations, or purposes specified by the donor(s) to the endowment." "Endowments," National Council of Nonprofits, accessed December 19, 2018, https://www.councilofnonprofits.org/tools-resources /endowments.

17. This article gives cost breakdowns for all types of the institutions we discussed in chapter 2: Megan Adams, "What Really Drives College Costs?," EAB Academic Affairs Forum, February 4, 2016, accessed May 2, 2018, https://www.eab .com/research-and-insights/academic-affairs-forum/expert-insights/2016/what -really-drives-college-costs.

18. Jon Marcus, "The Reason behind Colleges' Ballooning Bureaucracies," *The Atlantic*, October 6, 2016, accessed May 13, 2018, https://www.theatlantic.com /education/archive/2016/10/ballooning-bureaucracies-shrinking-checkbooks /503066/.

19. Paul F. Campos, "The Real Reason College Tuition Costs So Much," *NYT*,

April 4, 2015, accessed April 30, 2018, https://www.nytimes.com/2015/04/05
/opinion/sunday/the-real-reason-college-tuition-costs-so-much.html?_r=2,.

20. Matt Reed, "Dear New York Times, a Reality Check about Public Higher
Education," *IHE*, April 5, 2015, accessed April 30, 2018, https://www.inside
highered.com/blogs/confessions-community-college-dean/dear-new-york
-times.

21. Benjamin Landy, "Don't Blame College Teachers for Rising Tuition,"
Century Foundation, September 11, 2013, accessed July 3, 2018, https://tcf.org
/content/commentary/graph-dont-blame-teachers-for-rising-college-tuition
/?session=1.

22. Robert Hiltonsmith, "A Terrible Explanation for Rising College Costs,"
Policyshop, April 10, 2015, accessed July 3, 2018, http://www.demos.org/blog/4/10
/15/terrible-explanation-rising-college-costs.

23. "Mythbusting 'Administrative Bloat' in Student Affairs," NASPA Public
Policy Division, July 20, 2016, accessed April 30, 2018, https://www.naspa.org
/constituent-groups/posts/Mythbusting-administrative-bloat.

24. Blumenstyk, *American Higher Education in Crisis?*, 90, has a helpful
summary of the factors contributing to rising costs, including student services
and information technology. See also Brian Rosenberg, "Are You in a 'BS Job'?
Thank You for Your Work. No, Really," *CHE*, May 29, 2018, accessed June 1, 2018,
https://www.chronicle.com/article/Are-You-in-a-BS-Job-/243522?cid=at&utm
_source=at&utm_medium=en&elqTrackId=99dba4054ee149b298a681a447fc1724
&elq=32a7dbe389c04045bd29be8302ce36b7&elqaid=19241&elqat=1&elqCampaign
Id=8747.

25. Robert Kelchen, "Is Administrative Bloat Really a Big Problem?,"
www.RobertKelchen.com (blog), May 10, 2018, accessed July 3, 2018, https://
robertkelchen.com/2018/05/10/is-administrative-bloat-a-problem/. Kelchen
discusses bloat and other topics related to administrative costs in his book *Higher
Education Accountability* (Baltimore: Johns Hopkins University Press, 2018).

26. *Drivers of the Rising Price of a College Education: Midwestern Higher
Education Compact Policy Report*, August 2018, accessed August 24, 2018, https://
www.mhec.org/sites/default/files/resources/mhec_affordability_series7_2018
0730_2.pdf.

27. The Hanover report also includes a lot of helpful information about how
internal reporting is done at various institutions and methods for assessing
the financial health of institutions. "Financial Reporting in Higher Education,"
Hanover Research, October 2014, accessed May 4, 2018, https://www.hanover
research.com/media/Financial-Reporting-in-Higher-Education.pdf.

28. "Stanford Administrative Guide. Section 3.1.2: University Funds," Stanford

University, accessed May 4, 2018, https://adminguide.stanford.edu/chapter-3/subchapter-1/policy-3-1-2.

29. Marjorie Valbrun, "NACUBO Report Finds Tuition Discounting Again," *IHE*, April 30, 2018, accessed November 16, 2018, https://www.insidehighered.com/news/2018/04/30/nacubo-report-finds-tuition-discounting-again.

30. Colleen Flaherty, "Opportunity or Exploitation? Southern Illinois Carbondale's Proposal That Alumni Volunteers Do Faculty Work (without Pay) Doesn't Go Over Well," *IHE*, April 25, 2018, accessed May 2, 2018, https://www.insidehighered.com/news/2018/04/25/southern-illinois-proposal-alumni-volunteers-do-faculty-work-doesnt-go-over-well.

31. EAB is an organization that has pursued a number of ideas along these lines. See, for example, "Illuminate Your Underutilized Instructional Resources," August 9, 2017, accessed May 2, 2018, https://www.eab.com/technology/academic-performance-solutions/resources/infographics/instructional-capacity.

32. Ricardo Azziz, "Implementing Shared Services in Higher Education," *University Business*, August 18, 2014, accessed May 2, 2018, https://www.universitybusiness.com/article/shared-services.

33. Ry Rivard, "Shared Services Backlash," *IHE*, November 21, 2013, accessed May 2, 2018, https://www.insidehighered.com/news/2013/11/21/u-michigan-tries-save-money-staff-costs-meets-faculty-opposition.

34. "Lean Management," University of New Hampshire, accessed June 1, 2018, https://www.unh.edu/lean/.

35. Kristen Mitchell, "The 50-Year Agreement, OSU's $483M Parking Deal Stands Alone among Other Schools after Year 1," *The Lantern*, December 19, 2013, accessed May 2, 2018, https://www.thelantern.com/2013/12/50-year-agreement-osus-483m-parking-deal-stands-alone-among-schools-year-1/.

36. We explore UNC–Chapel Hill's recent bookstore outsourcing in chapter 9.

CHAPTER 9

1. Justin Stover, "There Is No Case for the Humanities, and Deep Down We Know Our Justifications for It Are Hollow," *CHE*, March 4, 2018, accessed March 9, 2018, https://www.chronicle.com/article/There-Is-No-Case-for-the/242724.

2. Richard M. Freeland, "Yes, Higher Ed Is a Business, but It's Also a Calling," *CHE*, March 18, 2018, accessed May 7, 2018, https://www.chronicle.com/article/Yes-Higher-Ed-Is-a-Business/242852.

3. Interview with Tim McGinley, March 27, 2018.

4. Freeland, "Yes, Higher Ed Is a Business."

5. Jane Stancill, "UNC Board's Approach Is All Business, and That Can Create an Uneasy Mix at Universities," *News and Observer*, May 18, 2018, updated May 19,

2018, accessed May 20, 2018, http://www.newsobserver.com/news/politics
-government/article211383694.html.

6. David W. Miles, "What One Trustee Wishes He Had Known Going In," *CHE*,
March 18, 2018, accessed May 7, 2018, https://www.chronicle.com/article/What
-One-Trustee-Wishes-He-Had/242840.

7. We are not implying that there is inherent conflict between businesspeople
and academics, although it is easy to find examples of it.

8. This perspective on collaboration was laid out in K. W. Thomas and R. H.
Kilmann, "Comparison of Four Instruments Measuring Conflict Behavior,"
Psychological Reports, 42 (1978): 1139–45.

9. Roger Fisher and William L. Ury, *Getting to Yes: Negotiating Agreement
without Giving In* (New York: Penguin, 1981).

10. David D. Perlmutter, "Lessons for Leaders Who Are 'Not One of Us,'" *CHE*,
April 1, 2018, accessed May 17, 2018, https://www.chronicle.com/article/Lessons
-for-Leaders-Who-Are/242928.

11. Email message from a colleague.

12. Susan Resnick Pierce, *On Being Presidential: A Guide for College and
University Leaders* (San Francisco: Jossey-Bass, 2012).

13. Paul W. Lawrence and Jay W. Lorsch, "Differentiation and Integration in
Complex Organizations," *Administrative Science Quarterly* 12, no. 1 (1967): 1–47.

14. All quotes are from Lawrence and Lorsch, "Differentiation and Integration
in Complex Organizations," 3–4, 4, 2.

15. Vivian Hunt, Dennis Layton, and Sarah Prince, "Why Diversity Matters,"
McKinsey & Company, January 2015, accessed May 18, 2018, https://www
.mckinsey.com/business-functions/organization/our-insights/why-diversity
-matters.

16. Rocio Lorenzo and Martin Reeves, "How and Where Diversity Drives
Financial Performance," *Harvard Business Review*, January 2018, accessed May
18, 2018, https://hbr.org/2018/01/how-and-where-diversity-drives-financial
-performance.

17. Stanford Graduate Business School staff, "Diversity and Work Group
Performance," *Insights*, November 1, 1999, accessed May 18, 2018, https://www.gsb
.stanford.edu/insights/diversity-work-group-performance.

18. Michael Watkins, *The First 90 Days: Proven Strategies for Getting Up to Speed
Faster and Smarter* (Cambridge, Mass.: Harvard Business Review Press, 2013).

19. Thanks to Laurie Wilder of Parker Search for emphasizing this point in our
interview, April 5, 2018.

20. Thanks to UNC Kenan-Flagler Business School dean Doug Shackelford for
sharing this anecdote.

21. This expression is often attributed to Winston Churchill, but see Richard M. Langworth, "Bull in a China Shop," March 13, 2009, accessed May 23, 2018, https://richardlangworth.com/bull-in-a-china-shop.

22. For a strongly worded argument on this front, see James V. Koch, "No College Kid Needs a Water Park to Study," *NYT*, January 8, 2018, accessed May 22, 2018, https://www.nytimes.com/2018/01/09/opinion/trustees-tuition-lazy-rivers.html.

23. Thanks to Jim Roth of Huron Consulting for this suggestion.

24. This point was suggested by Dean Doug Shackelford.

25. Liz DiMarco Weinmann, "10 Steps to Lead College Presidents Away from the Edge," *CHE*, April 10, 2018, accessed May 23, 2018, https://www.chronicle.com/article/10-Steps-to-Lead-College/243081.

26. Perlmutter, "Lessons for Leaders Who Are 'Not One of Us.'"

27. See "Josephus Daniels Student Stores," *Names in Brick and Stone: Histories from UNC's Built Landscape*, UNC–Chapel Hill, accessed January 2, 2019, http://unchistory.web.unc.edu/building-narratives/josephus-daniels-student-stores/. This site also references a *Daily Tar Heel* story from 2015, http://www.dailytarheel.com/article/2015/10/protesters-marched-to-folts-office-to-oppose-privatization-of-unc-student-stores.

28. This section is primarily based on 2018 interviews with university financial administrator Brad Ives and faculty members Lloyd Kramer and Beverly Taylor, as well as on our own peripheral involvement in the initiative.

29. Molly Looman, "The Pit and the Pendulum: University Icon Marks Social Changes through Time," *Daily Tar Heel*, December 23, 2018, accessed May 31, 2018, http://www.dailytarheel.com/article/2018/02/thepit-dth125–0222.

30. "UNC Considering Taking Student Stores Private," *Carolina Alumni Review*, October 5, 2015, accessed May 29, 2018, https://alumni.unc.edu/news/unc-considering-taking-student-stores-private/.

31. "UNC Considering Taking Student Stores Private."

32. Interview with Brad Ives, May 21, 2018.

33. All quotes from Professors Kramer and Taylor are from interviews with them on May 23, 2018.

Index

Page numbers in *italics* refer to illustrations.

College Access Index, 36–37
College of Arts and Sciences/College of Liberal Arts, 49–50, *50*, 100
College of William & Mary, 32, 161n3
Collins, Jim, 9, 98
commercialization, 110, 123–25
communications, strategic, 13
community colleges, 31
compensation, 93–94
competition, 27–28
conflict management, 140–41
Congress, 67
consortiums, 48
Constitution, U.S., 53, 64
consulting firms, 7, 29–30, 101
contingent faculty, 92. *See also* adjunct faculty
corporatization of higher education, 30, 95, 107, 148, 157n25
correspondence courses, 61
Council on Undergraduate Research, 60
course evaluations, 86, 174n16
credentials, 53
cross-functional: teams, 141
Crow, Michael, 24
curriculum, 55–56, 165n10; general education (gen ed), 53–54
curriculum vitae, 165n10, 172n7
customers, 17–18; students as, 30

deans, 17, 96, 99, 100–101; associate deans, *99*; faculty selection committee for, 105
decision-making, 3–4, 19, 28, 29, 103–4; mission-oriented as less effective, 13
degrees, 53–55; bachelor of arts (BA), 53; bachelor of science (BS), 53; bachelor's, 53–54; doctor of philosophy (PhD), 11, 55; master's, 54–55
department heads, 17, 96, 99, 100, 101, 102–3
Department of Defense, 67
Department of Education (ED), 65, 76, 131

Department of Health and Human Services, 67, 114
Department of State, 66–67
Department of Veterans Affairs, 67
departments, 49–50, *50*
development officers, 6, *97*
DeVos, Betsy, 66
differences between businesses and universities, 12–24, *24*; affiliation and loyalty, 19–21; chain of command, 16–17; goals, 12–16, 145; growth, attitudes about, 23–24; nature of work and guarantor of quality, 21–23; urgency, sense of, 17–19, 158n9
disciplines, academic, 19, 22–23, 97
discount rates, 25–26
dissertation, 83–84
dissertation committee, 82
distinguished professorships, 25, 91
diversity, 141–42
Dixon v. Alabama State Board of Education, 71
doctoral/professional universities, 37, 37–38, 39
doctoral thesis. *See* dissertation
doctoral universities, 32, 37, 37–38, 39
doctor of philosophy (PhD) degrees, 11, 55, 80–81; adviser matching process, 82; as apprenticeships, 80–81; coursework, 81–82; dissertation committee, 82; job search, 84–85; mental health disorders, 85; proposal defense, 83; research, transition to, 82–83; research focus, 86; teaching focus, 86–87; thesis defense, 83. *See also* PhD programs
doctor of philosophy (PhD) programs and degrees, 18, 37
Doe v. University of Michigan, 73
donors, 6; competition for, 28
due process, 71
dysfunctional institutions, 140

Eau Claire State Normal School, 41
Eisenhower, Dwight D., 159n17

Employee Forum (UNC), 148
endowments, 34, 35, *44*, 47, 116, 127, 130, 162n14, 184n16
Engines of Innovation (Thorp and Goldstein), 123
enrollment: selectivity, 23
enrollment numbers, 1; high school students, dwindling numbers, 2
entrepreneurs, faculty, 124–25
Equal Protection Clause, 69
ETOB (every tub on its own bottom), 129–30, 177n10
European Works Councils, 106
executive branch, 65–67

facilities, 133–34
facilities and administrative costs (or F&A), 117–18
faculty, 11; adjunct, 51, 91–92, 135; arts and humanities, 109; assistant professors, 85, 90; associate professors, 85, 87, 90–91; authority, *105*; chain of command and, 17; curriculum and, 55–56; dismissal, 88; distinguished professorships, 25, 91; fixed-term professors, 87, 91–92; full professors, 85, 90–91; governance, 103–6; hiring, 26; motivations, 94–95; non-tenure-track, 11, 107, 135; payment and salaries, 93–94; process for becoming, 80–85; responsibilities, 89–90; retention, 25–26; "rookie," 26; teaching loads, 92–93; tenure-track, 11, 84, 85–90, 174n15; types, 85–93
faculty-centric university, 107–9
faculty governance, 55
faculty selection committee, 105
faculty senate, 6, 105–6
failure, rates of, 18
Family Educational Rights and Privacy Act (FERPA), 75, 172n49
federal influence on higher education, 64–73, 96; admissions policies, 68–71; costs of compliance, 133; ex-ecutive branch, 65–67; free speech, 71–73; judicial branch, 68–73; legislative branch, 67–68; student rights to due process, 71
fighting words, 72
finance officers, 97
Financial Accounting Standards Board (FASB), 134
financial aid, federal, 76
financial crisis of 2008, 75
financial position, 135–36
financial reporting, 134–35, 185n27
First Amendment, 71–73
First 90 Days, The (Watkins), 143
first-year seminars, 57
Fisher, Abigail, 70–71
Fisher I (2013), 70
Fisher II (2016), 70–71
fixed-term professors, 87, 91–92; research-active faculty, 92
flipped classroom, 57–58, *59*, 62
Follett (retailer), 147–50
for-profit institutions, 31, 65
Forsyth County, Georgia v. The Nationalist Movement, 72
Foundation for Individual Rights in Education, 73, 78
Fourteenth Amendment, 69, 70
four-year institutions, nonprofit, 31; Carnegie Classification categories, 37–39, 164n35
freedom of information laws, 75–76
Freeland, Richard, 138–39
free speech, 71–73, 171n32
Free Speech on Campus (Chemerinsky and Gillman), 73
Friday, William, 33
Fulbright Program, 66–67
full professors, 85, 90–91
full-time equivalent (FTE) student, 7
funding: administrative bloat, 131–34; annual fund gifts, 127–28; arts and humanities, 116; capital budgeting, 130; endowments, 34, 35, *44*, 47, 116,

127, 130, 162n14, 184n16; overhead payments, 117–18; for PhD students, 82; philanthropy, 6, 127–28; private foundations, 116–17; provosts and, 100; of research, 11, 21, 113–18; sources, 126–28; spending, 130; by states, 7, 34–35, 74–75. *See also* grants

Gallogly, James L., 6
Gardner Institute, 57
Gates, Robert M., 78, 96, 106
general counsel, 97
general education (gen ed) curriculum, 53–54, 55
Generally Accepted Accounting Principles (GAAP), 134
Gerber, Larry, 107
GI Bill, 67–68
Gillman, Howard, 73
Ginsberg, Benjamin, 107, 108
goals of businesses and universities, 10, 12–16, 145
Goldstein, Buck, 123
Gonzaga University, 45–46, *46*, 47, 164n35; Center for Global Engagement, 52; funding, 128; governance, 105
Good to Great (Collins), 9
Google Scholar, 122
governance, 74, 96–98, 103–6; decline, 106–7; faculty senate, 105–6
Governance Reconsidered (Pierce), 6
Governmental Accounting Standards Board (GASB), 134
graduate students, 50, 81
grants, 52; Research Project Grant (R01, NIH), 115, 121; summer salary, 93; teaching load and, 93. *See also* funding
Gratz v. Bollinger, 69
Great American University, The (Cole), 125
Great Recession, 7

Great Society Agenda, 68
growth, 4; attitudes about, 23–24
Grutter, Barbara, 69–70
Grutter v. Bollinger, 69–70
guilds, disciplines as, 22–23

Handfield-Jones, Helen, 25
Hanover Research, 134
harassment, 72–73, 168n11
Harvard University, 32
hate speech, 73
Hendrickson, Robert M., 18, 22, 64, 99
higher education. *See* universities
Higher Education Act of 1965, 68
high-impact educational practices, 57
Hiltonsmith, Robert, 131–32
hiring, 9, 26
Hirsch index, 121, 122
historically black colleges and universities, 38–39, 67, 116, 169n15
human resources, 97, 174n13

imminent lawless action, 72
inclusion, 141–42
incremental budget model, 129
"indefinite tenure," 88
influences on higher education, 11, 64, 96, 145–46; accreditation, 55, 76–78; additional influences, 78–79; federal, 64–73; state, 73–76
information technology, 57, 133
infrastructure support, 117–18
Inside Higher Ed, 6, 25
Integrated Postsecondary Education Data System (IPEDS), 65
integration, 140–41
intellectual property, 11, 120, 124, 182n33
interactive classrooms, 58
interdependence, 22
interdisciplinary work, 52–53
intrinsic motivation, 112
inventions, 123–24, 182n33
invisible colleges (small private colleges), 18

professors. *See* faculty

profit, 23; as business goal, 12–14; as means to end in universities, 14–16; return-on-investment calculation, 28–29

program heads, *99*

promotion, 86

promotion and tenure review letter, 122

provost, *99*, 99–100

provosts, 17, 95, *97*; faculty retention as responsibility, 25–26

public and private institutions compared, 31–39; Carnegie Classification, *37*, 37–39, 130, 164n35; mission, 32–33; prestige and rankings, 36; size, 33–34; state support, 34–35; tuition and fees, 35–36; wealth, 34

publication, 110

public funding, 7

public good, 89

public policy, 78–79

public universities, 31–39, 161n3; examples, 40–43; mission, 32–33; state influence on, 73–76; United States Air Force Academy, 41–43, *42*, *44*, 49; University of North Carolina at Chapel Hill, *40*, 40–41, *44*; University of Wisconsin–Eau Claire, 41, *42*, *44*, 49

publishing houses, 119–20

"publish or perish," 121

quality, prestige, and reputation, 13–16, *14*, 97; rankings, 14–16

race as factor in admissions, 68–71, 170n23

rankings, 14–16, 27, 29, 36, 64, 158n6, 161n32

Reed, Matt, 131

Reeves, Martin, 142

referees. *See* peer review

Regents of the University of California v. Bakke, 69, 70

regulations, 65–67; "regulatory cap-

ture," 77–78; reporting requirements, 75; sunshine laws, 75, 143; Title IX, 65–66

"regulatory capture," 77–78

religious-affiliated schools, 39

reputation, 13–16, *14*, 22, 27, 97; professional service firms, 30

research, 9–11, 182n31; biomedical, 110–11, 113–15; in business world, 22; commercialization of, 110, 123–25; connected to field, not employer, 20; evaluation of, 120–22; examples, 110–12; federal influence on, 67; freedom in, 89; funding, 11, 21, 113–18; nature of work and quality, 21–22; publication of, 118–20; reasons for, 112–13; time as a cost of, 113

research grants, 4

research-intensive universities, 110; teaching, 90–91, 92–93

Research Program Project Grants, 115

Research Project Grant (R01, NIH), 115, 121

research seminars, 25

Research to Revenue (Rose and Patterson), 123

Research Triangle, 40

research universities, 40–41

resources, 28–29

Responsibility Center Management (RCM) model, 129–30

revision (revise and resubmit, R&R), 119

"rich get richer" element, 13, 15

Roosevelt, Franklin D., 68

Rose, Don, 123

routinization, 19, 22

royalty-sharing, 124

safety and security, 68, 133, 169n20

sales representatives, 7

Schoenbach, Lisi, 12

scholarships, 127

scientific research, 111–12

Scott, Robert A., 25

technology transfer offices, 123–24

tenure, 4, 50, 175n19; academic freedom and, 89; defined, 87–88; process, 85–90; publication and, 121

tenure-track faculty, 84, 85–90, 174n15

Texas A&M system, 74, 78

Thorp, Holden, 123

Tierney, William, 104

time orientation, 141, 159n10

Title IV of the Higher Education Act, 68

Title IX of the Education Amendments (1972), 65–66, 72–73, 133

Title VI of the Civil Rights Act (1964), 72

Toppo, Greg, 38

trade associations, 20

tribal colleges, 32, 116

"true threats," 72

Trump administration, 66

trustees, 89. *See also* boards

truth, search for, 89

tuition and fees, 35–36; discounting, 25–26, 126–27, 135; increase in, 131–32; PhDs exempt, 81; state regulation of, 75

tuition waivers, 81

two-year institutions, nonprofit: private, 31; public, 31

undergraduate experiences, 8–9

undergraduate research, 60

United States Air Force Academy, 41–43, *42, 44*, 50; Center for Character and Leadership Development, 52–53; governance, 105

universities, 155n4; constituencies, 13; differences among, 11; lack of interdependence, 22; large, 24, 33–34, 162n9; longevity, 10; multiple roles, 138; public service expectations for, 2; rankings, 14–16. *See also* American colleges and universities; collaboration between business and universities; differences between businesses and universities; private universities; public universities; similarities between businesses and universities

University of California, Davis, 69

University of California system, 74, 163n25

University of Central Florida, 24

University of Georgia, 32, 161n3

University of Maine, 2

University of Michigan, 69–70, 74

University of Michigan Board of Regents, 74

University of Missouri at Columbia, 8

University of New Hampshire, 38, 136

University of North Carolina, 25–26, 161n3; outside partnerships, 148; Student Stores, 147–52, *149*

University of North Carolina at Chapel Hill, 32, *40*, 40–41, *44*; Carolina Population Center, 52; deans, hiring of, 105; fixed-term teaching faculty, 91–92; funding, 127, 128; Greenlaw 101 flipped classroom, 58, *59*

University of North Carolina System Board of Governors, 139

University of Oklahoma, 6

University of Pittsburgh, 52

University of Texas at Austin, 70–71

University of Texas system, 74

University of Virginia, 75

University of Wisconsin–Eau Claire, 41, *42, 44*, 49, 74; Center for Communication Disorders, 52; service learning requirement, 59–60

"up or out" decisions, 87

urgency, sense of, 17–19, 158n9

U.S. News & World Report rankings, 14, 15, 36

Valbrun, Marjorie, 25–26

Vanderbilt University, 67, 130

Veblen, Thorstein, 8

Very High Research universities, 38

veterans, 67–68

Virginia v. Black, 72

"war for talent," 25–26
Warren, Earl, 69
Watkins, Michael, 143
Watts v. United States, 72
Wayland, Francis, 8
Web of Science, 122
Weinmann, Liz DiMarco, 146

Wente, Susan, 130
Whittington, Keith, 7, 89
Whorf, Benjamin, 108
work ethic, 95
worldviews, 23

Yale University, 32